Martin's love affair with flying machines began on weekend trips home from boarding school.

The man of my dreams

A special place for a special question

Our wedding in
Kansas City, Missouri

Whenever Martin was in the air, I was at the radio, maintaining contact.

Jeffrey and I often visited Dad's "workplace"—the hangar.

Jeffrey and me; I was barefoot, happy, and dressed as a Kankanaey tribal woman.

Flying with Daddy was such a special treat.

Mindy and Jeff worked on their homeschool assignments as preschooler Zach (foreground) looked on.

Filipino children loved the man with the red-and-white airplane.

In the tribal areas where we worked, kids come up with their own ways to have fun. In the background stands a typical tribal home.

When villagers noticed Martin's wet shoes every time he crossed the creek, they volunteered to build what they affectionately called "the Burnham Bridge."

One of Martin's responsibilities was transporting patients to medical facilities.

Martin and me on our porch in Aritao

Dos Palmas Resort

Our first "proof of life" photo, taken in July 2001.
Sabaya is in full jihad regalia, Martin is wearing a scrub from the
Lamitan hospital, and I'm in my one-and-only long-sleeved shirt.

Zach, Mindy, and Jeff continued a family tradition of documenting each
Father's Day. This photo actually reached us in the jungle, and we carried
it with us for the remainder of our captivity.

When Calvary Bible College named us "Alumni of the Year" in absentia, Martin's parents (left) and mine accepted the plaque in Kansas City.

My sister Mary in the Radyo Agong studio to make her appeal. When this photo was taken, we were fewer than twenty-five miles away!

...S Citizens
May 27

4 Harakatul Islamia
Targeting U.S. citizens

Bus Support of Israel in...
P.

① Oppression of muslims like...
② Sanctions against Iraq
③ Continued presence of Western troops in S...
Support RP govt in Muslim Island

Regards military ops...
be stopped and...
If understand that...
I'm good and...
assists in my...
as why not with us...
going...

Promises of God — I will never leave thee / He careth for you / Will supply all your needs
I'll prepare a place for you / Will come again / Honor parents + your days will be long / If you confess...
He will cleanse & forgive / Ask + it shall be given to you / He that believeth in me, the dead shall live
Acknowledge Him + He'll direct your path / If any man open the door, I will come in + sup of him
I've loved you w/everlasting love / When He appeareth, we'll be like Him / He'll perform a good work
I will not leave you comfortless, I will come to you / And lo, I am with you always / He that
believeth in me shall not perish but have everlasting life / Delight in the Lord and He'll give you the
desires of your heart / Vengeance is God's. He'll repay / Nothing is too hard for me

...all ye lands. Serve the Lord with gladness...
...me before his presence with singing. Know ye that the Lord, He is God. It...
...e that hath made us and not we ourselves. We are His people and the
...heep of His pasture. Enter into His gates with thanksgiving, and into His
...courts with praise. Be thankful unto Him, and bless His name, for the
Lord is good. His mercy is everlasting and His truth endureth to
all generations. PS 100

The Lord is my shepherd, I shall not want. He maketh me...
green pastures. He leadeth me beside the still waters. He...
He leadeth me in paths of righteousness for His names...
...through I walk through the valley of the shadow of d...
no evil, for thou art with me. Thy rod and thy...
me. Thou preparest a table before me in the presenc...
thou anointest my head with oil. My cup run...
goodness and mercy shall follow me all the...
I will dwell in the house of the Lord forever. PS...

Highest priority when getting home is to reconnect: w/ the k...
Need to recognize and respect the role that others have ha...
in their lives and not snatch them away. Our parents will...
also need some time. There are going to be alot of deman...
on us and setting priorities is going to be difficult.
Sometimes we're going to do it wrong. Keep going.

...s to the man who...the council
...the ungodly, nor standeth...the way of
...nor sitteth in the seat of the scornful
...his delight is in the law of the Lord and
...in his law doth he meditate day and night
...shall be like a tree planted by the rivers
...of water, that bringeth forth his fruit in
...his season. His leaf also shall not wither
...and whatsoever he doeth shall prosper.
The ungodly are not so but are like the ch...
...which the wind driveth away. Therefore
...ungodly shall not stand in the judgment...
...nor sinners in the congregation of
...righteous. For the Lord know...
...the way of the righteous...
...but the way of the...
ungodly shall perish.

Surely He hath borne our griefs + carried our sorrows...
A man of sorrows + acquainted with grief...
And we hid as it were our faces from him
He was despised and rejected and we did esteem Him
stricken of God.

Create in me a clean heart, O God. And renew a
right spirit within me. Cast me not away
from thy presence, O God And take not
thy Holy Spirit from me. Restore unto
me the joy of my salvation...

Hey my cool Parents,
We are having fun here
Grandpa and all our cousins.
...to rent + movies just now.
I didn't really enjoy the movie
thats ok. I just wanted to say
I'm looking forward to seeing y...
praying for you. Bye

Jeff
(the cool one)

Dear Mom + Dad,
I am doing good. I am staying with grandma +
grandpa. All my cousins are here also. Yesterday
I went to the animal clinic and I helped wash the
dogs and brush them and I helped play with the
cats. They had two dogs named Mo and Molley
they were brother and sister. They were part golden
retriever. I think. They were really friendly dogs. One
strong. Aunt Felicia showed me her cats. Her
some of them were nice and some were mean. One
would crawl into your lap and purr, her name was
Mona cat. I want her. She has a very good time
Fred. he is cute + I had a really good time
here. Well I have to go. I just wanted to know
I am praying for you. Bye Mom, bye Dad.
Love always,
Mindy
P.S. Happy Fathers Day dad.

...Mom and dad,
...I am fine. We went to
...is fun here. Mega
...computer games.
I will write you back.
Love, Zach

...me comes from
the heart
It's color matters not
Tradition says "It shou...
be red"
But white is all I've go...

Romance in the jungle...
...ship, my adored...
...citing lives we lea...

...re usually bored...
...I verse can not...

...of my affection
...der it an 'IOU'
...ty sweet
...ect

So dearer...
when w...
Better tim...
'I Love You',...
mine!
From Mart...
xxx

Happy Valentin...
Day, Mar...

I LUV U

Various writings that we
saved during our year of captivity

MGA KIDNAPPER!
MGA MAMAMATAY-TAO!

Abu Sabaya

Hamsiraji Sali

Khadafi Janjalani

Abu Solaiman

Isnilon Hapilon

PREMYO PARA SA IMPORMASYON
HANGGANG $5,000,000

The U.S. Government is offering a reward of up to $5,000,000 for information leading to the arrest or conviction of the terrorists responsible for the kidnapping of Martin and Gracia Burnham, and the kidnapping and murder of Guillermo Sobero. If you have any information about any individuals committing acts of international terrorism against U.S. persons or property, please contact the U.S. Embassy.

PREMYO PARA SA KATARUNGAN

www.rewardsforjustice.net

1-800-10-739-2737 (Manila)   1-800-877-3927 (USA)

Kung cell phone ang gagamitin ay tumawag lamang sa 02-526-9832/9833/9834

LAHAT NG IMPORMASYON NA MATATANGGAP NAMIN AY ITUTURING SIKRETO

The U.S. government offered a reward to pressure the Abu Sayyaf leadership. (Isnilon Hapilon is Musab's given name. Hamsiraji Sali is not mentioned in the book because we knew him only briefly. We called him Hamsi.)

Sheila (from left), Fe, and Angie celebrated their freedom in Manila. Our captivity continued another six and a half months after this photo was taken.

Ediborah Yap (center, seated) in happier days at the Lamitan hospital where she worked

SPECIAL EDITION

The Wichita Eagle

JUNE 7, 2002

50 cents

www.kansas.com

■ GRACIA BURNHAM MOVED TO HOSPITAL

■ WHITE HOUSE CALLS FAMILY IN ROSE HILL

■ BURNHAM FAMILY THANKS COMMUNITY FOR SUPPORT

MARTIN BURNHAM KILLED; WIFE GRACIA RESCUED

Filipino nurse also dies in firefight with rebels

Within hours of being rescued, I arrived at the U.S. embassy in Manila.

Woman to woman: President Gloria Macapagal-Arroyo wanted to hear the story of my rescue and Martin's death.

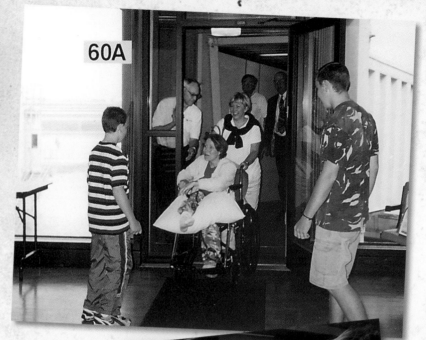

Home at last! Zach (striped shirt) and Jeff met me at the Kansas City airport. My sister Mary was my wheelchair driver.

My wonderful, all-grown-up daughter, Mindy

It was so good to see everyone at the groundbreaking for the new home being built for us in Rose Hill.

The Burnham family gathers to celebrate Zach's graduation in 2009. From left to right, Andy Hedvall, Mindy (Burnham) Hedvall, Gracia Burnham, Zach Burnham, Sarah (Neu) Burnham, and Jeff Burnham.

In Loving Memory of

Martin Burnham

High Flight

Oh, I have slipped the surly bonds of earth
And danced the skies on laughter-silvered wings;
Sunward I've climbed, and
joined the tumbling mirth
Of sun-split clouds - - and
done a hundred things
You have not dreamed of - -
wheeled and soared and swung
High in the sunlit silence.
Hov'ring there,
I've chased the shouting wind
along, and flung
My eager craft through
footless halls of air.
Up, up the long, delirious
burning blue,
I've topped the windswept
heights with easy grace
Where never lark, or even eagle flew.
And, while with silent, lifting mind I've trod
The high untrespassed sanctity of space,
Put out my hand, and touched the face of God.

John Gillespie Magee, Jr.
September 3, 1941

The funeral program included this quote from Martin's last message in his home church: "I wasn't called to be a missionary. I wasn't called to the Philippines. I was just called to follow Christ and that's what I'm doing."

Of course, Martin and I added, "You tell them out there that somebody needs to do something for us. Somebody needs to pay our ransom."

We had by then settled the debate—in our minds, anyway—of whether that was the right thing to ask. Martin had reasoned, "It is not our responsibility to figure out how a ransom payment is used. If we can trust the Lord for a million dollars, which is something totally beyond our reach, we can trust the Lord that that million dollars never buys a weapon or blows anybody up. These guys can just as easily send the money to their wives so they can live in luxury or something."

At the very last minute, Musab decided he wasn't going to let Ediborah go. He was a stubborn man and very proud. I think the only reason he made her stay was to show the group that he was the emir, the boss, and what he said went.

After many hugs and tears, the group began to make their way down the hill. But an hour later, they were back; they'd spotted soldiers at the bottom of the hill.

We mobiled to a different place where civilians were found who were willing to take the group into town. So we said good-bye again. I just wept when they left. I was happy for them, but I knew I was losing the companionship of girls I'd come to love.

Three or four hours later, they came back again! The civilians had failed to find out what time the jeepney left for town. So they would have to try again early the next morning.

We put up hammocks for the night. Martin and I were assigned a place right in the middle of all the activity—in fact, it was between two trees and directly over a big trash pile of banana peels, coconut husks, and marang skins left from cooking. Somebody decided this was a good place for our hammock. The flies were horrible. This only depressed me all the more.

Early the next morning when the girls left again, I cried, but I didn't make any more speeches or give them hugs. I just kind of waved at them as they went by. I thought about Job, of whom the

Bible says, "He sat down among the ashes" after his whole life had crashed (Job 2:8, KJV). That is exactly what I was doing.

Everyone was very quiet the rest of that day. The excitement in the air turned into a real sadness. I could tell that Omar missed Sheila right away.

Meanwhile, the thought began to dig into my mind that maybe, just maybe, this kind of a day would never come for us. After all, time was passing by. Every scheme that had gotten our hopes up had dwindled away. What was it Solaiman had said back on the speedboat that first afternoon? "We will make demands, and we will deal with you last." We were indeed left for last now, along with Ediborah. The rustling of the wind in the jungle trees only reinforced the loneliness in my heart.

15
THE PACKAGE
(Mid-November–Mid-December 2001)

EDIBORAH AND I HAD not spent all that much time together up to this point. My social life had seemed to revolve more around the needs of Fe and Angie. All this changed now that Ediborah and I were the only two women left in the camp, surrounded by some forty male captors.

A capable woman about my age, mother of four, Ediborah had been a nurse supervisor at the Lamitan hospital. Her husband had left her shortly after the birth of their last child, a son, six years before. She talked most about her oldest son, Jonathan, twenty-four, and how reliable he was. He worked for a fishing company in Zamboanga and sent or brought money home whenever he could. I could tell she was really proud of him.

Ediborah and I both needed to get our minds off the fact that we (along with Martin) were the last remnant now, so we volunteered for jobs. The guys had stolen a cow and her calf and had begun to butcher them—a skill they seemed to just naturally know, like tying your shoes. I'd never done anything like this, but Ediborah had, and so we said we'd cut up the meat.

That was easier said than done, because *bolos* were in short supply, especially sharp ones. We worked together that day, with me holding the meat while she sliced it thin, so we could then salt it and smoke it on the fire to preserve it. We actually had a good time.

I wondered to myself, *Now how does stealing this beef fit into the* mujahideen *code? I thought they didn't do that.*

Musab came around at one point, and I decided to ask him. Ediborah interpreted my words into the local dialect so he would understand better.

His answer was simple: "The civilian is nothing; the normal person is nothing. The *mujaheed* must go on." In other words, the fighter in holy war must have what he needs, regardless of the ramifications.

I pressed Ediborah a bit more. "But what if you get to the point of having an all-Muslim state? If people steal a cow in that situation, they would get their hand chopped off whether they're *mujahideen* or not, right?"

Her next answer was classic. "If we need it, it's not really stealing."

I thought back to June, at the Lamitan hospital, when hostages began looting that patient room of its supplies. The logic had been the same. Human nature seems to find ways to justify its wrongdoing, to move ahead with what serves its self-interests, and then to figure out an explanation so it doesn't sound so bad.

By the time Ediborah and I finished working with the meat, our hands were covered with blood, and we were sweaty. "Let's go to the river for a bath," she suggested.

"Well, sometimes they won't let us." The guys often didn't like to stop what they were doing and stand guard down at the river.

"They'll let us go," she said. "Just come with me and don't even ask." With that, she started off, and some of the guys scrambled to follow, as required.

November 19
President Arroyo arrives in Washington to assure President Bush that her military can handle the rescue. She also has lunch with Rep. Todd Tiahrt, who comes away "optimistic."

November 19
Jeff attends his team's football banquet.

• • •

The month of Ramadan had begun, when Muslims are allowed to eat only before sunup and after sundown. That rule didn't apply to Martin and me, of course; they didn't care when we ate. They called us to the fire before sunup to get our food, and we just saved it until later. We ate half of it for breakfast and the other half for lunch. Then we ate supper with the group after sundown.

The odd thing was, although Ramadan is called a time of fasting, these Muslims ate *more* during this lunar month. Food preparation started in the early afternoon, and they were very meticulous about their cooking. They wanted to have everything ready right at dusk, so they could promptly "break the fast." They looked at their watches time and again, and they discussed whose watch was correct. But they all waited for the leadership's signal that it was dark enough to begin eating.

We began noticing that when they were divvying up the budget, they fixed extra treats, like bananas mixed with sugar, but we only got our normal little pile of rice. "We can't give you any of this," they said. "It's for us because we're fasting—so we need more." The logic of that always seemed to escape me.

But then speaking of treats—a day or so later, a box arrived for Martin and me! I was over at the fire with Ediborah when she said, "The emir has some glasses for Martin."

"What did you say?!" I thought I had misunderstood her.

"A package came in for you last night. The emir has your eyeglasses."

I went dashing off to find that box, because I knew if I didn't claim it right away, it would be pilfered by the Abu Sayyaf. If it had any food in it, I knew I couldn't depend anymore on them stopping to screen the ingredients for shortening; they were too hungry now. I had to find that box immediately.

Sabaya had it. "Is that box for us?" I eagerly asked, even though I could see the New Tribes Mission marking on the outside.

"Yes, it is. But I have to look through it, because it might have some kind of microchip or homing device in it, so they'll know where we are."

"Sabaya, trust me—our mission would never do that!"

"Well, I have to look through it." With that, he turned away. A crowd began gathering around him.

I went back to where Martin was just being unchained from the tree after a night of sleep. "Martin, a box came in for us last night. They're going through it right now. Maybe you'd better go over there and claim it, or there is going to be nothing left!"

He immediately headed that way. When he got close, Sabaya said, "Oh, don't come over here; we'll bring the box to you."

"I just want to make sure that we get it," Martin said, standing his ground. Sure enough, he saw items starting to be removed from the box. One of the guys was already holding a package of Snickers bars.

Meanwhile, I went to get the glasses from Musab. He handed them over, a new pair from the same optician as before. When Martin put them on, a big smile came across his face; he could see clearly again, after so long! We were both so thankful.

In time, Sabaya finally brought us the box. "I had to take out the Cheez Whiz, because I really like that stuff," he said with a smile. "But the bulk of everything is still here for you."

We sat in our hammock and began pulling out our treasures—everything from cookies and crackers and peanut butter and bouillon cubes and soup mixes to letters and pictures. There was a *Newsweek* magazine with a cover story about the U.S. military buildup in Afghanistan. It had pictures of the weaponry they used—such as night-vision goggles and various guns. We knew the Abu Sayyaf would be interested in seeing the pictures even if they couldn't read the articles.

November 21
President Arroyo calls Martin's parents in Kansas to express her concern.

We began making little piles of all the wonderful things. But at the same time, we couldn't stop thinking about those Snickers bars. The bounty we had wasn't quite enough somehow. And then we looked at each other and said, "You know, this box has arrived from our mission out of nowhere—and we're complaining about what the Abu Sayyaf took? We should be rejoicing in the Lord's goodness."

We decided we needed to share. Martin began going from group to group, giving out spices, soup mixes, and cookies. I gave one of the two deodorants to Ediborah, plus some peanuts. She was very happy, and so were the others.

All of a sudden, Martin and I looked at each other again and realized something incredible: It was Thursday, November 22— Thanksgiving Day! We had asked the Lord earlier in the month to send us something nice for Thanksgiving, and he had done it!

Of course, I had asked for things before—a gift for Martin on his birthday—and been disappointed. So I hadn't really expected God to do anything this time. But here was a whole box of food, and it was so humbling. The Lord showed us he could bless us even when we didn't have any faith. How we enjoyed that package!

We were a little apprehensive that the *Newsweek* might cause trouble as people began seeing how well-prepared the American troops were for battle. But it had the opposite effect. The guys eagerly passed the magazine from one to another, studying the pictures and even ripping out some of them to save. They were totally intrigued. Martin and I had to fight to get to read the articles ourselves.

By now, of course, President Arroyo had made her U.S. trip, and we were still alive instead of in body bags in the cargo bay of her plane, as Sabaya had threatened. Actually, she had said earlier

---

November 22–24
The Burnham children spend Thanksgiving with Grandpa and Grandma Jones in Arkansas.

on the radio that she would be escorting us back home as her gift to the American government. It sounded good to the Filipino audience, but obviously, it hadn't happened.

Over the months, we had heard so many rumors about our being ransomed. But because the president of a country said, "They are almost out; I'm going to take them to the States with me," we couldn't help but hope.

A day or two after Thanksgiving, she came back on the radio to report that her time in Washington had been very productive, and she had called our parents to say we would be home by Christmas. We just laughed when we heard that. We knew it wasn't going to happen.

• • •

That Saturday, the guys brought in some *gabi*, which is a kind of stalk with a leaf on it, similar to rhubarb, only three or four times bigger. They cut it up and boiled it, then poured off the water because it was poisonous, then put in new water and boiled it again. *Gabi* is similar to cassava, which has a high arsenic content; if it's not fixed right, it'll kill you.

That night, the cooks must have been in a hurry and taken a shortcut, because while I was eating, my mouth began to itch, and my tongue started swelling. This had happened once before with *gabi*. I knew to back off immediately.

During the night, I woke up with severe chest pains. I wondered if I was having a heart attack. Then I thought back to the *gabi* at suppertime. I lay awake for much of that night and was glad I hadn't eaten more.

Early the next morning, which was Sunday, Sabaya called us

November 30
Bryant Gumbel of CBS's *The Early Show* does a live interview with Martin's mother, daughter, and sister-in-law.

---

over to say, "We've got a television reporter coming in. You are going to do an interview."

This was interesting. We didn't know whether to be glad or apprehensive.

"This is your chance to let the world know what poor condition you're in," he continued, "and that they need to ransom you. Gracia, if you could cry a little bit and be upset, that would help."

I looked at him and said, "How many days recently have I *not* cried?"

"Oh, yeah. That will be no problem for you."

Sabaya went on to tell Martin to mention two mediators: Sairin Karno, the Malaysian ex-senator, and somebody named Yusuf Hamdan. He rattled off those names like I'd say John Smith. Martin replied, "Well, when I start talking to a camera, I'm not going to remember." So Sabaya grabbed a piece of paper and wrote out the names.

Within minutes we were ushered down the hill. On the way, I thought to myself, *This could be good. Maybe we'll get to say happy birthday to Zachary!* He would turn eleven in a couple of weeks, on December 13.

Waiting for us was a young woman in khaki pants and an Adidas sweatshirt, with her head appropriately covered, of course. She had no film crew; instead, she held a small video camera in her left hand. She introduced herself. "Hello, I'm Arlyn de la Cruz from Net 25 television."

I gave her a hug and said, "Thank you for coming." I was struck in that moment that someone like this had actually been able to find us! The AFP had been trying for six months, and all of a sudden, here was a TV reporter right in front of my face. What I didn't know at the time was that this young woman was a personal friend of Janjalani's. She prided herself on getting into dangerous places and coming out with gutsy, award-winning interviews.

Accompanying her was a man named Alvin Siglos, a boyhood friend of Sabaya's. He stood around the edges taking his own home videos.

The Abu Sayyaf, meanwhile, encircled us like a choir, brandishing their weapons. The heavy-gauge barrel of an M57 mortar was intentionally placed right over Martin's shoulder. Sabaya stood with arms folded across his black shirt with the "No Fear" logo—a fitting mark for him—ready to throw in comments along the way.

Martin looked gaunt in his brown plaid pullover shirt and brown *pantos*. When he spoke, he clearly articulated the message that we were in desperate straits and needed help. "I would say to my own government," he said, "could you negotiate or talk to these people?"

Throughout the interview, his tone was controlled, almost flat, without flair of any kind. He seemed to be conveying to the viewer, *I'm walking a real tightrope here. I'm not telling you the tenth of it, but . . . fill in the blanks, okay?*

Meanwhile, I did what Sabaya wanted me to do and what I felt inside: I let my emotions show. My voice quivered at times as I said, "We're always hungry; there's never enough food. This is no way to live. There's no way to take care of yourself. . . . We've been forgotten. We need someone to show us some mercy. Is there no one in this whole country who can help us?"

After the interview, Arlyn went over to sit by Sabaya's hammock for more conversation. Martin and I went back to our place.

"I really just want to talk to her for a while," I told Martin. "There's so much I want to say off camera."

"Then go over there. Tell Sabaya you want to talk to her, woman to woman. He'll understand that."

I did. We began to visit. Arlyn also promised me a day at a spa when I got out. I told her I'd never been to one and would look forward to it.

She told us that September 11 had really hurt our chances, because now the U.S. was mad at terrorists and would never pay anything. As far as other sources of money were concerned, the stakes had grown too big for ransom. And besides, the Philippine

generals and government officials would need their cut. It was not very encouraging news.

She was hungry, and it felt good to be able to share crackers and peanut butter with her. She clearly sympathized with how awful our plight was. She ended up giving me a red sweater. I gave her letters to forward to our families. We had written them just in case we got a chance to send them out with someone.

While there, I learned that a new plan was being hatched. Sabaya said, "Arlyn, you can go out and sell this footage to CNN or some network for at least a million dollars—maybe two million. Just send it back to us directly for their ransom, and then we can let them go. You'll get to be famous, we'll get paid—everybody will be happy."

Sounded good to me! (None of us knew in that moment, of course, that the market value of the interview was not nearly so huge. CBS ended up paying fifty thousand dollars.)

"Even if I can't sell this to some foreign media," Arlyn added, "maybe my church, Iglesia ni Cristo, could help me put something together to help you." This is an indigenous denomination that's very large, with some unusual doctrines; for example, they believe that when Christ returns, not only will they rise to meet him but their *buildings* will go up as well, all of which have the same architecture across the Philippines. Attendance at weekly services is mandatory, complete with a sign-in procedure for enforcement.

Soon the reporter was gone, and we immediately mobiled out of that place, in case the military found out what had occurred. Would this interview get anyone's attention? So many other attempts had produced nothing to this point. We didn't expect miracles, that was for sure.

December 7
Arlyn de la Cruz's jungle interview airs on Net 25 in the Philippines.

December 11
Mindy's school Christmas concert is held. A special video tribute is given to the victims of 9/11 as well as Martin and Gracia.

• • •

The longer Ramadan goes on, the more irritable its observers become from the odd eating schedule. Someone told us that in some Islamic countries, there's a lot of road rage and street brawls near the end. It's as if people are just sick of the regimen.

I guess during Ramadan, you're also not supposed to have sex—although maybe that rule is like eating and applies only to daytime hours. Musab loaned me a rule book once that outlined all the requirements for those who disobey. I had to chuckle at one that said, "If you inadvertently have sex during Ramadan, here's what you have to do to make it right."

I looked at Martin and said, "Excuse me, but how does a person inadvertently have sex? I don't know!"

Meanwhile, of course, earning points with Allah had to go on. One day a captor named Lukman brought Martin and me a huge plate of bananas boiled in coconut milk. "Thank you!" we exclaimed. "How nice of you!" We assumed this was an act of alms-giving on his part.

It got to the point that there just was not enough food to support everyone. We were all scrounging for nutrition. At one point we had nothing but *carabao* hide for three straight days. They put the skin into the fire to burn it, then scraped it to remove the hair and soften it up, then burned it again, then scraped it again, over and over. At last they cut it up into chunks with a *bolo,* then boiled it for a long time.

What all this effort produces is a hunk of fat with extremely chewy skin on it. But by the time we put salt on it, it didn't taste as bad as it sounds. Of course, when a person is extremely hungry . . .

I found a piece of paper and, for the first time, began making some daily notes, like a journal. It was mainly a record of how long we walked, whether it rained or not, what food we managed to get, and how we slept. On Thursday, December 13, which was our son

Zach's birthday, I recorded, "I feel like a dirty animal—muddy, wet, stinky. Asked God for a nice place to take a bath."

A day or two before, a delegation had been sent out to get budget. In the process, however, they had met up with the AFP. One person was killed, and a couple of others were separated from us for a while. The rest came back empty-handed. Now we would have nothing.

On that Thursday morning, I said to Martin, "It's Wednesday night in the States—midweek service time in at least some churches. People are praying for us right now."

"Yes, that's true," he replied.

Just then another group of guys came into the camp. They had leftovers from the night before. But they weren't allowed to eat them during the day—so they gave them to us! I believe God answered prayer to relieve our hunger that day.

Finally, we got to the last day of Ramadan, which calls for a huge feast. We had walked for three days straight, from early morning to late at night, to get to a certain farm that would have plenty of fruit and vegetables, they said. At last we came to the top of a hill, and there it was.

This farm even had a well, which made it possible for us to have our first bath in four weeks. Ediborah shared some of her soap with us. Everybody was in a much better mood.

We began preparing a feast. One of the guys brought a kind of large, light green squash to me, with a *bolo* knife. "Peel this and cut it up," he said.

I looked at the huge *bolo* and thought to myself, *How is this supposed to work on this squash?* Obviously, I had no cutting board, and I could just see myself cutting off my finger trying to wield this big blade.

December 13
Zach's eleventh birthday. CBS manages to attend the party. Zach has to blow out his candles four times for the camera.

Someone had given us a spoon with a fairly sharp edge on it. Retrieving the spoon from my pack, I was able to skin the squash. It wasn't a pretty sight by the time I finished, but at least the job got done.

And once the sun set that Friday, we enjoyed a wonderful meal for a change. The only thing was, it was cloudy that night, obscuring the moon, so Ramadan was not officially finished after all. We got to do it all again Saturday night.

Martin and I were sharing a toothbrush, which didn't make for the best dental hygiene. When one of us got sores in our mouth, soon the other got them, too. My tongue always seemed to be sore. I don't know if it was caused by stress, lack of nutrition, or getting burned by the hot coffee because I was too hungry to let it cool down.

We finally learned to skip brushing if we thought we were just going to make the other person miserable.

I knew we needed to be flossing, too—but with what? We realized we could accomplish this by unraveling the rice sacks, which were made from a woven plastic fiber.

Water purity was not exactly a refined science. More than once we noticed that our rice tasted like soap, because one of the cooks had grabbed a pail of water from the same area of the river where people were bathing.

A popular shampoo brand in the Philippines is Sunsilk. We'd say to each other, "Hmmm—this is very good rice, with just a hint of Sunsilk!" Or, "This *viand* [anything that goes on top of rice, like a sauce] is really good, with just a sprinkle of Tide."

In fact, Martin's humor released my tension more than once. One day as we were walking along a river, I could hear Martin humming to himself. When we got to the next stop, I asked, "What song were you singing back there?" expecting to hear some great anthem of the faith.

"Theme song from *The Beverly Hillbillies!*" he replied. We both broke up laughing.

On another day, we were climbing a hill, and when we reached the summit, I was totally exhausted. I flopped down on the grass to cry. Martin looked at me, and instead of trying once again to comfort me with profound sentiments, he pulled a line out of a comedy routine by the Christian comedian and singer Mark Lowry in which he mimics a talk-show announcer: "What happens when two women love the same man, and that man is reaaally ugly? Stay tuned—we'll be right back!"

With tears still wet on my face, I absolutely split up. We just howled there on the hilltop and started telling each other more Mark Lowry jokes. I'm sure the Abu Sayyaf were wondering what on earth had happened to the American woman—she normally sits and weeps because her heart is broken and she's dead tired, but this time she's cackling!

Another time Martin entertained me by retelling a movie he had seen on his most recent long, trans-Pacific flight—only after all the big setup, he wouldn't tell me the ending. I was going crazy— "Come on, Martin! Finish the story!"

He never would.

16
SILENT NIGHTS

(Mid-December 2001–Mid-January 2002)

CHRISTMAS WAS NOW ONLY ten days away, although we had no outward reason to look forward to its coming. Our kids at home were no doubt busy with school concerts and parties and shopping—we could only imagine. We expected the twenty-fifth of December to be just another day of rugged mobiling through the steamy jungle.

About this time, Ediborah and I had several serious talks about Musab's pressuring her to get married. She always said, "Is it sinning for me to do this? I already have a husband [although she was estranged from him]. How can anyone have two? Of course, sooner or later, he's going to force me anyway."

As before with the other girls, there was no simple answer I could give.

Then late one night, somebody brought us some hot coffee and an *apam,* one of the little Muslim pancakes. How nice—a midnight snack! Sure enough, a day or so later, while Ediborah and I were making supper, she said, "Do you remember when they brought you the snack?"

"Yes."

"That was part of our marriage feast," she said with quiet resignation. "We're married now. Musab really wants to have a son."

"Well, Ediborah, you've done what you felt you needed to do."

The Abu Sayyaf had told her that this made her first marriage null and void, because her first husband had been a "Christian" (their term for any Filipino who wasn't Muslim).

It was hard to tell how sincere Ediborah's conversion to Islam really was. She told me she hadn't truly meant it in her heart. But then out came some phrase like "I do believe in the holiness of jihad"— whatever that meant. I looked back at her with big eyes and mainly kept quiet.

• • •

Sabaya, meanwhile, announced that he would be leaving us for a few days to get the negotiations "wrapped up." He was clearly unhappy that so many others had let him down: Solaiman, Doctora Rose, and even Arlyn de la Cruz, from whom nothing had been heard. Now he would go get a boat and take care of things himself.

As much as we tried not to think about it, Sabaya's trip did raise our hopes. Maybe President Arroyo's prediction that we would be out by Christmas was going to come true after all.

Several times he sent runners back to the camp with instructions for Martin to write a letter of complaint against Arlyn. The one dated December 21 read:

> *Martin,*
> *There is a good news you just wait for my announcement through Radyo Agong about your release.*
> *And regarding the letter of complain against Arlyn &* *Iglesia ni Cristo just do it.*
> *After your release just do something to help Alvin Siglos because Arlyn betrayed him after all the efforts he has done about your release, and you must also thanks to Sen. Sairin Karno because he is the real key of your release.*
> *A. Sabaya*

Martin composed a letter regarding the Arlyn de la Cruz matter as instructed, even though we didn't understand the deal and didn't see how it would help. It was carried out of the camp. Like so many other letters, we never saw any fruit from the effort.

• • •

At every new place, it was necessary to clear out underbrush in order to string up our hammocks and have space to cook. In fact, the Abu Sayyaf were notorious for whacking down all kinds of trees, whether it was necessary or not.

In one particular place, there was a tiny bamboo tree growing right beside our hammock space. Martin was ready to chop it down. I said, "Oh, wait, wait! Maybe that can be our Christmas tree." Not that we had anything with which to decorate it, but still it would have been a nice symbol.

Unfortunately, we ended up having to mobile out of that place before Christmas anyway.

On December 23, two of the group went out again—and returned with a packet of letters for us from the mission! Bob Meisel and Jody Crain from the NTM office in Manila had put together a wonderful assortment in a box, complete with an inventory list that showed everything from peanut butter to chocolate-chip cookies to cheese to soup mixes to magazines. But none of the items made it to us; apparently, Sabaya's group was enjoying them while out "negotiating" for us.

We read the list to Ediborah and talked about how different Christmas would have been had we gotten the box. But we didn't

December 19–21
Paul and Oreta Burnham and Mary Jones go back to Washington, again with New Tribes colleagues. Two of them, Kathy Ryff and Margie Clark, deliver a petition to the White House with more than twenty thousand signatures calling for the Burnhams' release.

mourn as before. We turned our attention to the letters, which were such a lift to our spirits—funny at times, poignant at others. Oreta Burnham had played stenographer for each of our kids, taking down their dictation so that we had a full single-spaced page from each of them. We found out the kids had gotten to go to my parents' place in Arkansas for Thanksgiving.

Mary, my little sister who lives in Ohio and is the spitfire of the family, hinted at her efforts with government officials to get some action: "I have lots to say. . . . We are working hard on this! Do you follow me? I want you to know that. Stuff is happening. You keep your chin up."

She also said she'd been to see our kids in Kansas. "I went to M[indy]'s basketball game this morning. She is also in the choir and has solos because of her great voice. She has good fashion sense and dresses cute. Z[ach] is a nut, and we have decided that we need to trade Z and myself [to the Abu Sayyaf] for you and Martin. We would drive everybody crazy, and be asked to leave!"

She also gave Martin and me an assignment: Think of appropriate boy and girl baby names, since she and her husband, Lance, were planning to start a family.

Martin's brother Brian and his wife, Arlita, wrote: "We feel guilty having so much when you are poor and hungry. . . . We wish we could send you a truckload of chocolate."

Our oldest, Jeff, after describing his football season, turned reflective: "I saw your videotape that the reporter took. I was happy to see your faces but VERY sad to see your condition. (Why do they cuff you, Dad?) . . . I want to tell you how proud I am of you. You guys are the best parents I could ask for. I'm looking forward to seeing you again. (By the way, Dad, that beard looks good on you.)"

A two-and-a-half-page, single-spaced letter from my niece, Sarah Tunis, included long quotations from Ephesians 1, James 4, Colossians 1, and Philippians 1, among others. This became our "Bible"—we read it every day.

Christmas Eve came, and I sat in the hammock singing carols,

while Martin gathered firewood. Normally, that was my job because he would already be chained. But on this evening, he volunteered for the job.

It had rained hard that afternoon. As rainwater ran off the *tolda,* we gathered it to drink. Then that night, we had *sindol,* which is hot coconut milk that can be mixed with a variety of things: chopped bananas, chopped sweet potatoes, pieces of coconut. We also had marang, a banana, and rice with *viand.*

Eating in the dark was always difficult, of course—but we couldn't start the fires until sundown, the time we knew any soldiers in the area would have stopped searching for us and returned to their tents.

The night was cold. Lying there, I heard a plane go over. I heard some of the guys still up, cooking "personal" food, and it made me very sad.

At midnight on Christmas Eve, the Philippine custom is to have a little feast. Guess what: Ediborah came over at midnight to bring us crackers and cheese! Wherever did she get them? I have no idea. But we were grateful for her generosity.

In previous years I had loved planning ahead for Martin's Christmas gifts. Whenever I heard him talk about an author he admired, I'd go write down the name lest I forget, so I could buy the book.

He liked cowboy stuff. One day, before our capture, I was walking down the street in Malaybalay and saw a shop called Chico Craft. In the window I saw beautiful carvings. That sparked an idea. I happened to be reading the *Little House on the Prairie* books to the kids at that time, and the front of each chapter had a woodcut of an old Western main-street facade.

December 24
Two million subscribers to *U.S. News & World Report* get the Burnham story, with a picture, as part of a three-page feature on Philippine terrorism entitled "Opening Up a Second Front."

I took this in to Chico Craft and asked, "Could you make a shelf to mount on the wall with three pegs underneath for hanging things, and on top a carving of this scene?"

"Oh, yes, we can do that." It turned out marvelously and took its place in our living room. Martin was so pleased with that gift.

This year in the jungle, however, I had to face the reality that I would have no gift for my husband at all.

When we awoke the next morning, breakfast was plain rice with nothing on top—not even salt. I had begun brushing up on the Christmas story from the Bible, which I had memorized as a kid. So I recited parts of Luke 2 for Martin that morning: "And she brought forth her firstborn son, and wrapped him in swaddling clothes, and laid him in a manger; because there was no room for them in the inn. . . ."

We reread our letters from our family and talked about what they would be doing on this special day. On Radyo Agong our captors heard greetings from both Doug and Brian Burnham and told us, which warmed our spirits. We took a piece of paper and drew a checkerboard on it, turning little twigs and pieces of foil we had saved into the light- and dark-colored pieces, so we could play the game. We spent a lot of time singing and praying and talking together.

Lunch turned out to be a bit of fish soup, hot tea, rice, and roasted bananas. Martin started not to feel well after that and took a nap. We heard artillery even on this day, but not close to us.

In America, the postholiday question when everyone returns to work or school or church is, "Did you have a good Christmas?"

Yes, Martin and I had a good Christmas. Why? (1) We had something to eat, and (2) we didn't have to pack up and hike. In our minds, that made the day positive.

• • •

On December 30 or so, word came that we were to mobile to a certain place to meet Sabaya and the others who had gone with him.

Every relocation, of course, meant finding a new spot for our hammock. Martin used to drive me crazy redoing it. He would get it all set up between two trees and then say, "Okay, why don't you sit down and test this?"

I'd sit down. "Fine—it feels really good."

"Well, it looks to me like this end is a little higher than the other end. Why don't you get up, and I'll retie it."

After this process was completed, I would again pronounce it perfect—and he'd say, "Well, I may have gotten that just a bit low. Could you stand up again? I'll retie it."

This would go on and on until I'd say, "Enough already! The hammock is fine. You're just like my brother-in-law Bill!"

A few years before, I had gone with Bill one day to shop for apples. At the first grocery store, we walked through the fruit section, and he must have picked up every apple to examine it, but ended up buying only four or five. Then we went to a few orchards, where he used the same scrutiny. He felt the apples and hemmed and hawed. Sometimes he bought a few, and sometimes none at all. It was hilarious.

Now in the jungle, I joked with Martin, "I hope you never go apple shopping with Bill. You two would take weeks and probably buy nothing!"

Every time after that, whenever I got annoyed with his perfectionism, I said, "Someday you and Bill are going to go shopping for apples!" And we'd laugh together.

December 26 and following
Christmas presents for Martin and Gracia remain unopened in a corner of the Burnham living room in Kansas.

December 28
The Joneses and Burnhams gather at the Kansas City home of Gracia's brother, Paul. The families have an extended prayer time for Martin and Gracia.

December 29–31
Rep. Todd Tiahrt travels to the Philippines to meet with President Arroyo and military leaders.

When we joined up with Sabaya, we learned that he had not been able to go to town as intended; too many soldiers were watching. But a negotiation was still proceeding, he claimed, and things were going to turn out fine regardless.

He told with some pleasure how the AFP had tried to poison him but failed. He had hired a man to get food for the group, and one day he had put in a request for fresh fish.

The man, however, had leaked this information to the military. The AFP had offered to provide the fish. The toxin they added had made the Abu Sayyaf members very sick. One of them named Bashir had almost died, in fact. But in the end, they were all alive to tell the story.

The next day we said good-bye to Moghira and another leader, Umbran, who took their groups off on a striking force. This left just fourteen of us: Ediborah, Martin, myself, and eleven captors.

While gathering up some marang under a tree, we noticed an unusual airplane overhead. It wasn't the kind that usually tracked across the Basilan sky. All eyes turned to Martin.

"Is that the kind that's going to bomb us?" people wanted to know.

"Oh, no. That's a twin-engine plane, the kind flown by a dignitary or someone very important."

Sabaya looked at us and said, "Well, on the radio I heard that your congressman is here from the United States, from Kansas."

We looked up again, longingly this time. Could it be that Representative Todd Tiahrt, our congressman from the Wichita area, was actually so near at hand? A warm feeling came over us. Maybe he would be able to bring about a breakthrough where so many others had failed.

That night Ediborah came up with special treats to welcome the new year: tiny pieces of cheese and some crackers. The next day, a newspaper arrived in the camp. A new letter had arrived from "them"—again, we didn't know who—requesting another "proof

of life." Sabaya somehow came up with a camera, and so we posed sitting together and holding up the newspaper with its date.

Martin had to show Sabaya how to load the film and where the shutter button was. With every attempt at pressing it, however, Sabaya jerked the camera wildly. We told him he needed to hold still, but we weren't very successful.

Ediborah posed with us for a couple of pictures, too.

• • •

The coming of the year 2002 meant that we no longer had a calendar. We'd been referring to the small 2001 pocket calendar I had rescued from our identification on the speedboat, but now we would have to keep track of the date in our heads. More than once there was disagreement in the camp about what day it really was. But Martin, with his organized mind, invariably turned out to be correct.

Soon the military pressure increased again, and we retreated inland to the higher elevations. One evening, as the sun was setting, we were going through our nightly routine before bedtime— I would put on an extra shirt and extra pair of pants; we'd brush our teeth; we'd pray together; Martin would carefully stow his glasses in their case for safekeeping—when suddenly, we heard wood being chopped not far away.

"*Sundalo!*" came the word. "Just on the other side of the hill!" They were chopping down trees and setting up their hammocks.

We very quietly packed up and took off in the opposite direction, down to a river and then along a trail.

There, in a quiet moment, we heard a soldier talking into his radio! Obviously, there were more soldiers in that direction, too. We just kept walking. Late that night, we stopped along a river for a few hours of sleep. Early the next morning, we moved on into the mountains, where we spent a relatively peaceful four or five weeks.

Martin and I gave this place a name—"Camp Contentment"— because that is what the Lord was teaching us there.

"You know," Martin said to me one day, "here in the mountains I've seen hatred; I've seen bitterness; I've seen greed; I've seen covetousness; I've seen wrongdoing." I nodded my head vigorously, thinking back to incidents I had observed as well.

But then he surprised me. He hadn't been talking about the Abu Sayyaf as I had assumed.

"I've seen each of these things in myself. The Lord has been showing me how incredibly sinful I am." He then proceeded to go back through the list.

"Hatred? At times I have hated these guys so strongly. When we were getting cheated out of food, I'd sit and think, *Wow, I wish I had a big pot of rice, and* they *were the ones chained to a tree. I'd sit there and eat it all in front of them.*

"At other times, when one of them pulled out a 'personal' snack from their stash and ate it, I coveted it rather than being happy for that person."

He kept going through the list. We talked about how our hearts are wicked, and how we had rationalized that by saying we were the ones being wronged and so our feelings were only "natural."

"But Jesus said to love your enemies . . . do good to those who hate you . . . pray for those who despitefully use you," Martin continued. "He said we were to be the servants of all—and he didn't add any exception clause like, 'except for terrorists, whom you have every right to hate.'

"Let's just ask the Lord to work out some contentment in our hearts and teach us what he wants us to learn."

We decided to do that. We committed our situation to the Lord.

January 2, 2002
The Philippine government accepts U.S. offer of "training and logistical support."

January 3
Martin's sister and brother-in-law, Walt and Cheryl Spicer, return to their teaching at Faith Academy in Manila.

I can't say we became models of saintliness after this. But we did get to the point where we could go stand at the fire and accept a lesser amount of food than everyone else without complaining or going back to our spot discussing our portion size. That had become a bad habit of ours, and we were able to stop it.

I saw Martin's servant heart with regard to one of the fellows we called "57," since it was his job to carry the M57 mortar. He seemed perpetually in a bad mood. I had said to Martin that I thought the name was fitting for him since he'd been a grouch for at least fifty-seven days in a row!

Only later did we find out that he suffered from chronic headaches.

Martin went over to him one day when he was sitting, just moaning from the pain. We had gotten some ibuprofen in a recent package, and Martin gave him one. "Here, this will help your head," he said. "I'm praying for you."

Not long after that, "57" was sent out on a mission of some kind. When he returned, he was totally different toward us. Even when he was cranky with others, he was always nice to us. Martin continued supplying him with pain reliever whenever he sensed the need.

• • •

This resolve to be content, however, was put to ever increasing tests. In mid-January when the radio reported that American military had arrived in the Philippines to help train the AFP, it really made Musab angry. He took it out on Martin by "forgetting" to send someone in the mornings to unchain him from the tree.

If Martin, however, asked to be freed in order to go to the bathroom in the woods, they freed him and did not rechain him afterwards. He found himself debating whether to say he had to go even if he didn't, just for the benefit of getting loose.

It got to the point where if Martin didn't say anything, he was chained twenty-four hours a day.

Meanwhile, I was really craving privacy, especially while going to the bathroom. Finally I dragged all the branches that people had chopped down while arranging their hammocks and formed a barrier up against a hill so Ediborah and I could avoid being watched. The only trouble was that the brush pile proved attractive to snakes. One day she showed me a snakeskin she had found.

I said with a touch of fatalism, "Well, good! If one of them bites me, that'll be the end of me, and I'll be outta here." At this point, death seemed a pretty good alternative to living the rest of my days as a hostage.

By then, both of us were getting so little to eat that our monthly periods ceased. In the earlier months there had been enough money to keep the women supplied with what they needed, and when anybody was ransomed out, she passed her supplies down to the ones remaining. Now the Abu Sayyaf were low on money—but it didn't matter anymore.

Ediborah was worried, however, that perhaps she had become pregnant, which Musab very much wanted. I told her, "Don't worry about it—my period has stopped, too. It's the lack of nutrition." In fact, I was right. Several months later, when the diet improved, our cycles resumed. Only then did we have to resort to using rags a few times.

As for toilet paper: I enjoyed a grand total of two rolls during the entire twelve months of captivity. I made them last as long as possible!

January 16
Brian and Arlita Burnham return to their mission work in Papua New Guinea.

January 17
Jeff calls Radyo Agong to wish his mother a happy birthday.

. . .

Staring at the same tree day after day after day, Martin started planning businesses he might launch if we ever got back to Kansas or Arkansas.

"What if I set up a flight school? Or what if I lined up weekend seminars for pilot certification?" He began estimating the income this might bring and the costs it would entail.

Several times Martin mentioned that when he got back to the States, he'd like to try to find the Taylorcraft single-engine plane that my dad had owned long ago. He wanted to buy it back if he could.

What about starting up a doughnut shop? We picked out a certain spot for it in the parking lot near the IGA and the Pizza Hut in Rose Hill.

One day we even talked about him running for mayor of Rose Hill! We outlined a campaign, complete with candidate qualities and local issues to be tackled. How about a town swimming pool? What would stimulate more business? It was stupid, given the fact that we'd never actually lived in Rose Hill but only stayed there during furloughs every five years or so.

On another day, Martin said, "Gracia, what would you think of me becoming a pastor?" That led to a long conversation. Soon he was telling me sermon ideas.

Sometimes we made vacation plans for our family. "Let's plan a camping trip out to the state park. We'll leave on Friday after the kids get out of school. Should we stay through the whole weekend, or should we come back in time for Sunday morning church?" We'd plan all the gear to take, what we would eat each meal—anything to occupy our minds.

Then on January 17, a Thursday, my birthday came. I had never expected to spend this day in the jungle. The Abu Sayyaf were aware of the occasion, and two days before, they had brought in a cake about ten inches across, baked in a special pan. We guessed that the

ingredients were probably about the same as those in pancake batter, except the cook had used Royal Orange soda for some of the liquid.

On my birthday, the group stretched one tiny 170-gram can of corned beef (about six ounces), imported from Brazil, over two meals. We couldn't believe how flavorful it was. It went well with rice and Maggi noodles. When it was time to cut the cake, we got our share—two little squares about two bites each.

We managed to rig up a windbreak of branches to ward off the cold. That night we invited Ediborah over so we could visit and talk about birthday traditions. We'd saved a mini-size Cloud 9 candy bar, which we cut up with my spoon into three pieces to share with her.

After she left, Martin and I prayed together and then went to sleep. It certainly wasn't like any other birthday I'd ever celebrated in my life. No balloons. No cards. No gifts. No bedroom door to close behind us for a romantic ending. But in its own modest way, it had been a nice day.

17

SO CLOSE

(Late January–Late March 2002)

ONE MORNING WHILE IN "Camp Contentment," Sabaya came up to me and asked, "Do you know someone named Mary Jones?"

My heart leaped. "Yes! That's my little sister!"

"Well, she's in Zamboanga, and she's going to make a statement on Radyo Agong soon. I'll bring my radio over so you can listen to it."

What in the world! My sister was just across the strait in Zamboanga City? I had never wanted so badly to fly like Superman in my life.

We huddled around the shortwave there under our *tolda*. Soon the announcer said, "We have today Mary Jones, sister of Gracia Burnham, who has a statement to make."

And there came the voice I knew so well. I listened intently with a big smile on my face as she spoke very forcefully for four or five minutes, expressing her concern for us. Our children were frightened after seeing the pictures of our deterioration, she said. She appealed to the Philippine government to do something. She also appealed to the Abu Sayyaf: "Please do not harm them. You have nothing to gain by doing so. They are peaceful people."

Then as she ended, she gave phone numbers for our captors to call.

"Wow!" I exclaimed to Sabaya. "Yep, that was my sister!" I turned to Martin and continued, "She said very nice things about

us, didn't she?" We both laughed at that. We couldn't believe that she had gone to all this effort and travel for us.

The next morning, Sabaya was back with a frown on his face. "They're airing part of her statement again—the part about the phone numbers. Why is she doing that?"

"I don't know," I replied. "Maybe she just wants to know how we are. Maybe she brought money with her." I figured that should get his attention.

He wasn't eager to respond, however. "Well, we don't have a sat-phone, so there's no way to call even if we wanted to. You write her a letter and ask what her real reason for coming was. Ask why she gave those phone numbers. Tell her we don't have communication, but in the meantime, Janjalani and Solaiman can speak for us; she can trust them.

"No one will see this but Mary," he added. "We will forward it to Alvin Siglos, who will take it to Manila and personally deliver it."

So I got some paper and began to write what I knew I was supposed to say:

Hello Mary,

It is the day after we heard you on the radio. Abu Sabaya came to us this morning. He is confused about your real purpose here in the Philippines. It is reported that you are being escorted by the FBI. You have given phone numbers to call. Does this

---

January 21
CBS airs a *48 Hours* feature built around Arlyn de la Cruz's footage taken back in November. Public concern in the U.S. heightens.

January 24
Six hundred sixty U.S. troops arrive in the southern Philippines.

January 24–30
Mary Jones and her husband travel to the Philippines, meet President Arroyo, and make an appeal on Radyo Agong for Martin and Gracia's release.

---

*mean that someone at these numbers is willing to negotiate with
the group for our release?*

*The group wants you to know that we will never be released
without some concession. Their losses have been great and they
will never just give us up. They are asking for the return of
their homeland, but since that seems impossible just now, they
are willing to take a ransom, as they need to arm themselves for
this fight.*

A couple of paragraphs later, however, I began to write more
personally out of my heart:

*Could you please send us a pkg. with Alvin? . . . Could you send
a couple thousand pesos [$40] for us personally so we can get
medicines, etc. I need boots. Martin gets thinner & thinner. It is
hard to watch, Mary!*

*This whole situation is so difficult. Everyone is being stub-
born . . . we are caught in the middle . . . the Abu Sayyaf will
not let us go w/out ransom . . . the governments say "no ransom." This is an endless circle, and to be honest, we do not want
to be rescued, as they come in shooting at us. If someone can't
give somewhere, we will die.*

*Thank you for coming here and reminding the world that we
are people . . . we are being treated as only political pawns and
it is very sad. You are kind and sweet. Tell Mom & Dad I love
them . . . and my kids. I love them so much it hurts.*

When I finished, Martin said, "Hey, I think I'll write
something."

"You're going to get us in trouble!" I warned. "Sabaya said to
keep it short."

"No way. I'm not letting this opportunity pass." So he added a
couple of pages. Among other things, he said:

It seems as though something should happen soon . . . but we've been saying that for a long time. We remain encouraged in the Lord. Many of you included Scripture in your last letters—they have become our Bible and we read them daily.

Jeff, Mindy, & Zach . . . it's hard to know what to tell you except I love you so much and am praying I can come home to you soon. Jeff, I wanted to watch the World Series, then the Super Bowl with you (and all the other bowl games), but I don't even know who played! Isn't that funny? Happy Birthday to you!

When we finished the letter, we took it to Sabaya. Later we discovered that it did *not* go directly to Alvin Siglos. It ended up at Radyo Agong and was read over the air before it ever got to Mary! I would not have been nearly so blunt had I known that would happen.

Needless to say, the Abu Sayyaf never called the phone numbers. Sabaya was too busy worrying about Mary's FBI agent. We should have told him that this was standard practice in any kidnapping case involving Americans; the FBI would have been involved from day one. But even that wouldn't have relieved his fears.

Not long afterward, one of the captors' wives showed up in camp with a story of having met Mary at a congressman's home in Isabela, the provincial capital of Basilan. She said Mary was crying, had "boxes of money," and was pleading for my release. It sounded good—but the truth, I found out in the end from Mary, was that she was never in Isabela at all. Zamboanga City was as close as she got.

• • •

Our food supply at this time was actually quite good for a most unusual reason: The armed forces were feeding us! A group of them met our guys and handed over quantities of rice, dried fish, coffee, and sugar. This happened several times over the course of a few weeks.

Why in the world did President Arroyo's troops provide the

Abu Sayyaf with their daily bread? We were told that it was because Sabaya was wheeling and dealing with the AFP general of that area over how to split up any ransom that might be paid. Arlyn de la Cruz had warned us about that. "You know, this is going to be a really big deal," she said, "and everybody is going to expect their share."

Sabaya was willing to give the general 20 percent of the action. But the messenger reported back that this wasn't enough. The general wanted 50 percent—when his own government steadfastly condemned the ransom concept altogether. We weren't really surprised at this, as over the years we had read newspaper articles about generals' wives installing floors of smuggled marble in Corinthian Gardens, an elite section of Manila, and about their children attending the best schools abroad. Those things don't happen on a Filipino general's salary.

We soon learned via radio that negotiations had broken down. Radyo Agong often uses coded messages in public-service bulletins. For example, if someone's father dies in the city, the station will let all the relatives and friends in the province know what has happened, since many don't have telephones.

One day, the announcer used a tip-off name for Sabaya and said, "The bank turned down your offer for the house that you wanted to sell, and they're going to come now and take the house by force. My advice would be for you to leave the house so you don't get in any trouble."

It didn't take too much sleuthing to figure out what that meant. Negotiations with the general had broken down, and we needed to move along.

Just at that time, another incident gave cause for relocating, too. Assad came running up the hill with the key to Martin's handcuffs and took them off. He was excited and talking nonstop, although we couldn't understand much of what he was saying. We figured out that our captors had caught a man who said he was out "looking for an ax" he had lost several years before.

But this fellow had found the Abu Sayyaf once before, and

Omar had warned him, "Don't you come looking for us again, or we'll kill you."

Now they sat and talked with him a long time. They finally decided he was a scout for the army. So after moving us over to one end of the camp, they took the prisoner up the hill and beheaded him. We didn't see or hear the actual event, but we saw Bashir coming back down the hill trying to get the blood off his shirt.

A little while later, Sabaya stopped to tell Martin all that had transpired. "I'm sure this kind of blows your mind," he added.

"Well, you know my views on it," Martin replied. "You know I believe it's wrong, even if you call it 'holy war.'"

Again came the standard explanation: "This was just this man's destiny. He should not have come looking for us. But he did, and now we have to find a new camp." This was what upset Sabaya most—the inconvenience of moving.

We remembered a recent conversation we'd had with Sabaya about a Muhammad Ali interview that had appeared in the December *Reader's Digest* we had gotten in our pre-Christmas box. The magazine's writer had been scheduled to talk to the famous American boxer at his Michigan home back on September 11, of all days. They went ahead with the interview that morning and of course the journalist began by asking Ali for his reaction to the attacks.

"Killing like that can never be justified," he had said. "It's unbelievable. I could never support hurting innocent men, women and children. Islam is a religion of peace. It does not promote terrorism or killing people."

The interviewer then asked how Ali felt about the claim being made already on the news that Muslims were responsible for the World Trade Center and Pentagon disasters.

"I am angry that the world sees a certain group of Islam followers who caused this destruction, but they are not real Muslims. They are racist fanatics who call themselves Muslims, permitting this murder of thousands."*

*Howard Bingham, "Face to Face with Muhammad Ali," *Reader's Digest* (December 2001): 92–93.

We showed the article to Sabaya and asked what he thought about it.

"Well, of course Muhammad Ali would denounce this; he's living the good life in America! As long as he has plenty of money, he's not going to say he agrees with us, because that would ruin his prospects.

"But I can assure you that if he's truly a Muslim, he knows about jihad, he understands jihad—and he appreciates jihad."

• • •

We walked for hours up the river where we had to be more careful than on a normal trail. We always had to take the hardest route, usually through thick foliage. We would see trails and know to avoid them, for fear of civilians spotting us. From a hilltop, the Abu Sayyaf would point out a village in the distance and say, "We're going over there. On the trail it would only take a few hours"—but we'd end up taking two days to get there, up and down, up and down.

We walked through water up to our waists, with mud and gunk at the bottom. We'd carry our boots rather than risk having them suctioned off.

We estimated that by this time, Martin was carrying close to fifty pounds of gear: his odds and ends of clothing, our hammock, the chain with which he was bound every night, some budget, plus one or two big mortar rounds, which they called "M90 mortars." These are canisters at least three feet long that fit into a mortar launcher. He came up with a long strip of cloth somewhere (perhaps from someone's discarded hammock) and tied it to each end of the "mortar," so he could sling it over his shoulder and thus have his hands free. A lot of times when scrambling up a hill in a steep place, we really needed our hands to grab onto a branch.

Meanwhile, I was carrying perhaps twenty-five pounds, including a couple of what they called "M60 mortars." These weighed four or five pounds each and were about the size of a Pringles can.

I noticed my arm and calf muscles getting very strong from all the exertion, even while the rest of my body was weakening.

And the crazy part was, these heavy "mortars" never got used! We just lugged them around the jungle week after week. In a firefight, there wasn't time to set them up and fire them; guys just grabbed their assault rifles and began blazing away.

Given the loads, Martin and I had more than one debate about which personal items were essential. Back in June when the schoolteachers had been so kind to me, they had given me a pair of jeans. But Martin asked me not to wear them, because Muslim men object to seeing a woman's figure; I was supposed to be in the baggiest thing possible.

So I stuck to *pantos* while still carrying the jeans around. After a couple of months, we discovered that Martin had lost so much weight that *he* could wear the jeans. He decided he wanted to hang on to these for his release day, whenever it came. He also had a nicer, heavier shirt with a collar he had been given at the hospital. Together, these made up his special outfit.

We carried those around for months. One day I said, "Martin, this is not going to be a quick captivity. We're carrying all this extra weight through the jungle; what do you think?"

"Man, I hate to get rid of them. I just keep thinking we're going to get out soon. If I could walk out of here looking decent, I'd really like it."

A few days later, though, we gave up and buried the jeans behind some rocks. He was very sad about this, and so was I. We kept the shirt, however, for warmth at night.

Sometime in February, as the food supply kept shrinking, I began noticing that when I sat up in the morning, I could feel the blood pulsing through my head, *boom—boom—boom!* That went on for weeks, until the diet improved again. I didn't know if my blood pressure had gone crazy or what. It was scary.

When I was really down and feeling sorry for myself, I would think about what I might have wished had never happened.

Did I wish our family had never come to the Philippines in the first place? No, we'd had a wonderful fifteen years before the capture.

Did I wish I'd never married Martin? Absolutely not.

Did I wish I'd never become a Christian when I was a little girl? No.

The only thing I could agree to wishing was that I'd never been born. I sounded like Job when he said in his agony, "May the day of my birth perish. . . . That day—may it turn to darkness; may God above not care about it; may no light shine upon it" (Job 3:3-4).

Obviously, my mental state was becoming shaky. Several times I said to Martin, "I would rather be dead than live anymore in this situation."

"Gracia, you can survive. What do you think the kids would say if you could pick up the phone and call them?"

I had to admit, "They'd say, 'Just keep going, Mom, because maybe you'll get to come home someday.'"

"That's right. And that's what you need to do. Don't let your mind think long-term. Just keep walking until the next rest break. All this will seem like such a little while after you're out."

Poor Martin—he was so good to put up with my emotions. If we were in a gun battle and I was falling apart, he would say, "Gracia, this isn't the time to cry. You're wasting energy. You need to get ahold of yourself—you can cry later, okay?"

But he never reprimanded me for crying. It made me think back to earlier days, when I was homeschooling the kids, and I pushed Jeffrey so hard to perform that he would burst into tears. On more than one occasion I had said, "I don't want to see you cry, because you're just trying to get your way." I was really impatient and unfair with him.

Now in the jungle, I thought to myself, *How would you feel if someone walked up to you right now and said, "I don't want you crying, because you're just trying to get your own way"*? I promised myself that if I ever got back to Jeff, I would sit him down and apologize for pushing him so hard. He was actually a good student, and

so were the other kids. I just expected them to be perfect little adults instead of kids who were learning to make their way in the world.

. . .

I also learned to lighten up a bit with one of the captors named Akmad. He was about fifteen years old, like our Jeff, only chunkier, and could be happy-go-lucky sometimes. But he was very moody at times—a normal teenage boy, I guess.

He found ways to divert our food to his own benefit. Sometimes he claimed that the group food was "personal." He was the one who had invented the strange line "You can't have any of this—we need this food, because we're fasting." (The Abu Sayyaf generally "fasted" on Mondays and Thursdays—during daylight hours, that is. They ate before sunrise and after sunset, of course.)

One day Akmad and a couple of others were chosen to supervise our bathing and laundry process at the river. We knew this wasn't a favorite job for them, so we tried to hurry up and do exactly as we were told. "Faster, faster!" Akmad barked. Soon he began throwing rocks at me to get me to hustle even more.

Upset, I swung around and said, "Okay, then I *won't* hurry! Go ahead and throw them at me!" He didn't understand all of my English, but the rocks kept coming.

Still not getting the results he wanted, he cocked his gun.

"Fine—go ahead and shoot me," I said. "I really don't care."

Fortunately, he didn't take me seriously, but the rock barrage continued until Martin finally said, "No! Don't do that!" Only then did he stop.

A few days later, Akmad happened to see a picture of our daughter, Mindy, who was only twelve. Of course, Filipina girls are small, and so Mindy appeared quite mature in Akmad's eyes. He began saying he'd like to marry her.

"No way," I replied, "after the way you've been treating me!"

Ediborah translated what I said to Akmad. He just grinned and

said back to her, "How do I tell her in English that I'm a 'good boy'?" She taught him the English phrase.

But whenever he tried to use it with me after that, he got confused. I'd go to the fire, and Akmad would say brightly, "You are a 'good boy'?"

I'd smile and say, "Yes, Akmad, you are a 'good boy.'"

He would then push his luck by saying another English term he'd learned from Ediborah: "Mother-in-law?" At this, everybody would laugh.

I would shrug my shoulders and say, "Maybe—if you are a 'good boy'! "

Several times when I saw him stealing dried fish, I'd scold him, "Akmad! You are a 'bad boy'!"

He would just smile at me and insist, "I am a 'good boy'!"

I remember thinking more than once, *This kid should be coming home from school to warm cookies and milk, not traipsing through the jungle with an M16.* Instead, he and the other young ones were more like the "lost boys" in *Peter Pan*. Martin and I even used that term for them once in a while when talking in the late evenings.

In a gun battle later on, Akmad ended up taking a bullet through his thigh. He could not just lie down, however; he had to run with the rest of us for quite a distance. We went through a swamp with water up to our waists, which of course infected the wound.

At the first chance to rest, I noticed some of the guys picking up leaves from the ground and putting them into their mouths to chew. I didn't know what this was all about until they then began stuffing the masticated leaves into Akmad's wound as some sort of medication. Martin and I gazed at this in disbelief and decided to keep quiet. Then the wound was bandaged to stop the bleeding.

Martin gave up his long *malong* for use as a stretcher. Akmad was then carried along the trail with the rest of us.

Before long, however, infection had produced a high fever. He began talking out of his head. Late one night, we heard him repeating himself over and over in his language. The only parts we

could understand were the intervals of *"Allah akbar! Allah akbar! Allah akbar!"* Then he began to growl in a low voice, "Personal! . . . Personal! . . . Personal!" I felt so sorry for this young man.

The days wore on, and there were too many soldiers in the area to risk sending Akmad out for medical help. His ranting became more frequent as his condition worsened. Naturally, he needed help going to the bathroom, and others were not always nearby to assist him.

One day, he had soiled his *malong* and sleeping mat, and I could see that he was upset.

"Hugasi bani?" I said in my fractured Cebuano, which means "May I wash this for you?"

He nodded.

I took the two items to the stream and washed them out. As I hung them up to dry, the thought came to me: *If this were Jeff, I'd want some lady to show kindness to him.*

• • •

Jeff's birthday (February 11) came and went, as did Valentine's Day. We tried to make cards for each other. In my log I wrote: "If we ever get out of here, Martin wants Valentine cookies (sugar) w/ frosting and cupcakes w/ frosting. . . . How I wish I could make him some. I love him so much—and we are hungry."

February 11
On Jeff's fifteenth birthday relatives gather for another party.

Mid-February
The Bush administration adopts a "subtle, but very important" shift in U.S. policy on civilian hostage situations, from "no deals at all" to case-by-case consideration, with an openness to ransom if it would in some way bring terrorists to justice.

February 21
A U.S. Chinook helicopter goes down in the sea off Zamboanga; ten soldiers die. The Abu Sayyaf hear this news and rejoice.

For the time being, however, we made do with the local snacks if they were available. The three "official goodies" of the Abu Sayyaf were:

- Magic Flakes, which are three saltine crackers with icing between
- Cloud 9, a candy bar sort of like a Milky Way, but with no shortening (or at least none listed in the ingredients)
- Bingo cookies, similar to Oreo cookies

Martin even kept the empty wrappers so he could smell them when there was nothing else to eat. The leftover aroma dampened his hunger pangs a little.

Meanwhile, we were learning to appreciate a different kind of delicacy: eel. The river had lots of eels, and the guys built beautiful fish traps with vines and other materials to catch them. Eel is really good to eat; it has a lot of fatty skin, and the meat is excellent. We thanked the Lord every time somebody brought us a slice of eel for supper.

We learned to avoid dried squid, however, which is something Filipinos seem to love. Martin quickly found out it made him very sick. One night they forgot to handcuff him for sleeping—which turned out to be convenient when he needed to go vomit in the woods. He was careful to call out, *"Sakit ako! Sakit ako!* [I'm sick! I'm sick!]" so they wouldn't think he was trying to escape and shoot him.

That was the last time we ate squid; from then on we skipped those particular meals.

The first few times I faced little dried fish, complete with heads and tails, I took off the head, then carefully picked the rest apart, throwing away each tiny bone in order to get at the meat. I then sprinkled the meat on our rice to give it flavor.

But as time went on and we began to starve, we decided the fish heads probably had good protein. Everyone else was eating them, and we started to as well, along with the bones of the skeleton—we just chomped down everything.

Sometimes bigger fish would come, and we would be given only the head. We learned to chew it up and be grateful for the nutrition. Fish-head bones are not as hard as one might think; the only part that can't really be crunched, believe it or not, is the eyeball. It's hard as a rock. Martin just swallowed his whole and let his stomach do the work. I couldn't make mine go down, so I'd throw it away.

One day about the time I did laundry for Akmad, I was at the babbling brook again. I looked down at a tiny pool formed by the rocks at the edge and saw a little fish about an inch and a half long.

I didn't think I could catch it, but I reached down anyway—and grabbed it by the tail. I held it up to Martin. "Look! I caught this fish!" I exclaimed, very proud of myself. "Do you want it?"

"No, that's okay."

So I popped it in my mouth and ate it raw. After all, if I carried it around with me until a cooking fire became available, it might rot. Better to get the nutrition now. In fact, it tasted very good. Who says God had to supply our needs the same way every time?

By now my hair was getting long and needed to be in a ponytail to stay out of my eyes. My *terong* wasn't enough to do the job. Obviously, I didn't have a scrunchie or a rubber band to use. What to do?

Lord, can you figure out something for me to use to tie back my hair? I began to pray. That may sound silly to others, but when we

---

Early March
Gracia's uncle approaches an American philanthropist for ransom money and gets a favorable response.

March 11
The Wall Street Journal runs a front-page article on the widening war against terrorism and reports, "The most ambitious U.S. military action outside Afghanistan is taking place on the small island of Basilan." The article attributes to U.S. officials the opinion that "the Philippine troops are poorly organized and have yet to learn how to move with the stealth and speed they need to rescue the Burnhams and Ms. [Ediborah] Yap."

had absolutely nothing, we learned to pray about things as mundane as this.

I was learning the truth of the Scripture that says, "Every good and perfect gift is from above, coming down from the Father" (James 1:17). If somebody walked by and handed us a tiny boiled banana only two inches long, our immediate response was *Oh, thank you, God! We need this.* Every bite was a gift.

Soon after, I glanced down at the ground—and there lay a strip of black rubber, like from a bicycle inner tube. I picked it up, tied the ends together in a knot, and gleefully pulled my hair back. This became my scrunchie for a long, long time.

When I lay down in the hammock on my back, however, I'd have to take it out to be comfortable. I was always afraid of losing it. So I would carefully stuff it into my pocket. I needed to guard this prized possession.

• • •

Sabaya had an unusual question one day: "Are there a million Christians in America?"

"Oh, certainly," Martin replied.

"Well, then, couldn't they give a dollar each and get you guys out of here?"

We just groaned. I said to Sabaya, "There are a lot of Americans in the States who wouldn't give you a single dollar, Sabaya. You are a bad guy, and people don't give their money to bad guys!"

He looked at me, shocked, as if to say, *What? Me? A bad guy?* This was preposterous, to his way of thinking.

Whenever he saw me upset or crying these days, he tried to patch me up by saying, "There's a negotiation! There's a negotiation!"

I wanted to reply bluntly, "No, Sabaya, there isn't. You've said that dozens of times now, and it's never produced anything." But I held my tongue.

18
RANSOMED!

(Late March–April 2002)

IF YOU'RE EVER TEMPTED to go camping in a swamp of mangrove trees—don't. Mangroves are fairly short tropical trees with much of their root system *above* the ground, forming a picturesque tangle of limbs that eventually converge into a trunk some three feet or more into the air. They flourish only in places with abundant water.

A mangrove swamp is a great place to hide, if a person doesn't mind the smell of rotting leaves and the dampness. We spent two nights in one just before Easter and about went crazy. When we got out of our hammock, our feet sank two inches into the goo.

Of course, I must admit it was a tiny improvement over the previous week, when we'd lived in bunkers the Abu Sayyaf had dug into a steep hilltop. With no more than five feet of head-room, we crouched in the darkness, forbidden to go outside for fear of discovery. Martin and I had to share a bunker with Musab and Ediborah, which meant I couldn't communicate openly with my husband. Martin seemed more depressed here than at any other time.

At least in the mangrove swamp, we could see the sun through the trees.

Being close to the ocean meant we weren't far from civilian fishing activity. In the Philippines, a common (although illegal)

way to catch fish is simply to throw a stick of dynamite into the water. When it explodes, the dead fish float to the surface, where the fishermen can collect them and take them to market. It's not exactly friendly to the environment, but it works.

Whenever we heard a big *ba-boom!* I cringed in fear of an incoming AFP mortar. The others calmly listened a few seconds, analyzing the sound, and then declared: "Fish bomb." In other words, no problem.

Another *ba-boom!* I held my breath and then someone else announced: "Fish bomb." I never did learn to tell the difference.

One evening, the guys who had gone out for budget came running back with news. Their excitement was obvious, even though we couldn't understand their dialect. Everyone quickly began packing up to mobile. My immediate thought was that soldiers had found us again. We began packing, too.

Then Martin looked at me and said, "You know, I don't think this is a soldier thing. People are too pleased about all this."

We hiked out of the swamp and came to where Sabaya and Musab had gone for a meeting. They had us sit down. Then they spoke.

"Someone has paid a ransom for you—15 million pesos [$330,000]. So this is really, really great."

At last! Our hopes had finally been realized. We'd be going home!

We both held our breath for the next line.

"But—we are going to ask for 30 million pesos more." They had always said they wanted a million dollars for Martin, and they were sticking to that figure.

I remembered, just a day or two before, hearing Sabaya on the phone telling someone in town, "Take anything they offer, because

---

March 14–19
FBI director Robert Mueller visits his Manila staff to review their efforts and to encourage action.

we are ready to get this over with." But now I studied their faces and could just see the hardness settling in.

"Please, please do not do that," I pleaded with Sabaya. "Take the money and let this be over!"

"No, no—the person who paid this ransom said that if we require more, they'll come up with it. This won't be a problem."

I thought to myself, *Well, okay, if that's true, go ahead and ask for the rest.* Meanwhile, all the Abu Sayyaf guys were celebrating. "The money's been paid, the money's been paid! You're going to get out of here! *Allah akbar!*"

"Okay, we're going to leave this island now," Sabaya said. We began an hour's walk toward the sandy beach, where we sat waiting for a boat while the captors kept several cell phones going.

Mosquitoes were everywhere, of course. I had a tiny bit of Off! in my backpack, but I didn't want to get it out for fear that the zipper would refuse to close again, as it often did. So we just sat there getting bitten.

In time, someone said, "The boat's here. Move up close to the shore." We heard the engine sound drawing near.

A spy plane was also circling overhead during all this. We had come to ignore them, however, because they had been circling for months, and nothing ever happened. "Why don't they do something useful with those things and spray for mosquitoes?" Martin said ruefully.

Someone gave a flashlight signal from the shore, and a small boat called a *banca,* maybe twenty or twenty-five feet long, pulled up. We began wading out to meet it in chest-deep water. We awkwardly pulled ourselves aboard and sat down. The Abu Sayyaf began loading their guns and bazookas on board, then climbed in themselves. Soon the boat was full, and more people kept coming.

I turned to Musab. "There are too many people on here; it's going to sink," I said. "You've got to get some of them off."

He looked at me like I was crazy.

But in fact, the boat began to take on water. People tried to bail

with their hands. I got a little bowl out of my backpack to help. Even Akmad was bailing with his hands from his *malong* stretcher as he said over and over, "No panic! No panic! No panic!" When they saw we were sinking, a number of guys disembarked.

The spy plane kept circling above. *If they can't see us now, they really are useless,* I thought to myself.

Finally, with some fifteen of us on board, the boat took off toward the bright lights of Zamboanga. This little, out-of-the-way island of Basilan had been our abode for ten months. Now at last, we were finally making headway toward freedom. I was so grateful. The open breeze was freeing for me, after so much hiding in foliage.

Several weeks earlier, I had gotten frustrated with praying for release; it just wasn't happening no matter how I prayed. So I had said, somewhat childishly, "Okay, I'm going to pray for something else: a hamburger!" I even told Martin what I was doing and said, "The only way for us to get a hamburger is to get out of here, right? Maybe God will answer that prayer instead!"

Now in the boat, Musab looked at me with a big smile and said, "We're going for your release!"

"Tonight? Will we be released tonight?"

"Oh, no, no. Maybe a week. Maybe two weeks. Maybe a few days."

My heart plunged. So this was not going to be our big moment after all. *Here we go again,* I thought. *Why did I let myself expect anything more?* It seemed that we were being toyed with once again.

• • •

We rode the waves all night. Poor Ediborah, who didn't swim, was terrified. Martin just held on to her hand and said, "We're going to be fine; we're going to be fine."

The Abu Sayyaf were not about to venture directly into Zamboanga City, of course, with its AFP Southern Command

headquarters and all the other security forces. They stayed in the shadows and worked with intermediaries.

By morning we had landed at what they called Island 11. A war between two tribes fighting over a water source was underway. The AFP generally stays out of such conflicts. Hence the Abu Sayyaf assumed we would be safe.

Most of the civilians had fled the island, leaving many abandoned houses for us to occupy. The available water was very sulfuric, and Martin and I both got sick right away. Diarrhea raged, and we vomited as well. Yet we weren't allowed outside, Sabaya said.

Well, that simply would not work, given our condition. So they moved us to a different house that had a bigger room. They put up a big tarp divider to keep us hidden from any visitors. Martin pried up a piece of the floor in order to make a place for our wastes. It was totally gross.

We found a big box of the absent homeowner's clothing that, I am sorry to admit, we basically stole to turn into rags and use as toilet paper. Occasionally the captors brought us water for washing.

Meanwhile, of course, money was still flowing freely—our ransom money. (After my return to America, I read various reports that the ransom money had been diverted and never reached our captors. Not true.) Every night a boat came from the mainland with supplies. Every captor had been given 10,000 pesos ($200) to spend as he wished.

Ayub, probably eighteen years old, spent a tenth of his wad on cookies! He had huge sacks of Bingo cookies and sat down for a feast.

Lukman spent a lot of his money on clothes, especially a few classy motorcycle shirts. A handsome fellow, his long, straight hair was quite striking.

One evening late, after the supply boat had come and gone, the room began to fill with the most wonderful smell as Martin and I sat behind the tarp. We peeked around the corner, and there was Assad

with a big tub of hot fried chicken! He looked up at us, grinned—and tossed us a thigh, like he would toss something to a dog!

"Oh, thank you, Assad!" we cried.

"I'm spending my money!" he said with glee.

He also bought a tape player and some music, which was supposedly "forbidden." When scolded for this by another captor, Assad told the fellow off and said, "Leave me alone—it's good Muslim music."

Soon the Abu Sayyaf came to realize that this island was not as safe as they had thought. The AFP might not be there, but the tribal war was just as dangerous. Word quickly got around that the Abu Sayyaf had arrived, and nighttime skirmishes flared up.

The first time, we had to leave our stuff behind and run out of the house for a while. Through the darkness we ran to the only cement structure on the island, where Martin and I slept on the floor in the far corner. No blanket, no *malong*, nothing to fold up as a pillow. That was a long night, especially with the gunfire continuing. Just before dawn, they sneaked us back to our house.

The next time hostilities broke loose, we began packing immediately. Someone came running into our room. "Get your things! We're going!" And soon we were loaded back onto another *banca*.

We were surprised to see a woman already on the boat when we got on. We were even more surprised when we learned it was Musab's first wife. Where had she come from? I had no idea. I didn't get a good look at her, because it was dark, and she was covered in black except for her face. She did have a baby girl with her.

In the middle of the night, we pulled up to a little Muslim fishing village near Zamboanga. They sneaked us under the houses built on stilts over the water and then hauled us onto a plank sidewalk

March 25
The Philippine military turns down an Abu Sayyaf offer to release a hostage in exchange for a temporary cease-fire and medical care for one of its commanders.

with a number of boards missing. We had to walk very carefully. I was barefoot, not wanting to lose my boots in the water.

When we got to a house, Ediborah was put into a room with us, while Musab and his wife were in another room.

Soon the Muslim call to prayer began ringing out across the village. It was mournful but also beautiful in a sense. When the sun came up, someone was dispatched to find breakfast. Oh, my! We had *banana-cue*—ripe banana pieces rolled in brown sugar and fried in oil. We had deep-fried doughnuts! We had ripe mangoes. What a feast! We were glad the Abu Sayyaf had lots of money again. The money hadn't gained our freedom, but at least it was improving our diet.

Even so, Musab couldn't bring himself to divide up the twelve doughnuts equitably. Martin and I received one each, while Musab kept the others.

Previously, when we had gone without adequate food for a time and then got relief, we tended to wolf things down too quickly. Food would get stuck in our esophagus, and we'd gag. We'd almost forgotten how to swallow.

This time we ate very slowly and chewed each bit a lot. I tried to make each mouthful last for forty chews, so my throat could swallow easily.

At lunchtime, there was fried chicken with rice! We had gravy for the rice, and some fruit salad.

For a snack that afternoon, we got *halo-halo,* which is crushed ice with sweetened condensed milk that has been mixed with fruit, sweet corn, and even garbanzo beans. It tasted so good!

The group called civilians to bring us freshly cooked fish. Twice a day, someone brought hot tea with sugar in it, as well as rice. We really enjoyed it.

Omar had brought his wife along on this journey, and during the day, she decided to go shopping. When she stopped by our sweltering little room to get Ediborah's list of items, however, she made a mistake. She had a friend with her, whom she carelessly

allowed to follow her into the room, thus exposing the presence of us two Americans. The captors became irate, and Omar's wife got a royal chewing out. She turned as white as a Filipina can turn.

For supper, they bought a hunk of beef, which was prepared over a small kerosene cookstove the Abu Sayyaf had bought. Again, we feasted.

Toward evening, Sabaya asked us, "Is there anything you'd like to have?"

"Well, Gracia's been praying for a hamburger," Martin offered.

"Hey, I'll send my guy to Jollibee [the Philippine counterpart to McDonald's]."

Sure enough, around nine o'clock, some hamburgers arrived with French fries and Cokes. We shared one with Ediborah—but that got her in trouble with Musab. After all, Jollibee hamburgers might have pork in them.

"You realize we're going to have to move now," Musab announced, "because a civilian saw you." Everyone began packing up, and guides from the local area were called to assist. I was swathed with *malong*s so as not to be identified.

Just before we left, something happened that simply broke my heart. Our group was still carrying along the injured young Akmad, who by now was growling and screaming a lot of the time. We could tell he was slowly losing his mind.

Ediborah, being a nurse, had been urging Musab to figure out some way to help the kid. After all, Akmad was his nephew. We joined in as well. "Somebody really needs to do something," we said. "Why is he continuing to suffer like this?"

"It is the will of Allah," came the response. "He has been confessing his sins: stealing food from the group, not saying his prayers, not reading his Koran. So this is Allah's punishment for him."

I wanted to scream back that the suffering had nothing to do with Allah; it was all the fault of the Abu Sayyaf leaders. They had control of Akmad's life.

Now, just as we were walking out of this house on stilts above

the ocean, I peeked in another room and caught my last glimpse of the boy. A baseball cap was pulled down over his eyes. He was so skinny I could see the bones of his elbows through his skin. His arms and feet were tied down to anchor points in the floor and wall, and a sock was tied into his mouth with a bandanna to gag him. He thrashed pitifully against the restraints.

My heart just went out to him. The irritation of weeks before when he had thrown rocks at me was long gone. I felt nothing but sorrow for the agony he was now enduring.

Later I was told that the AFP raided that house, captured him, and tried to question him. Where is Akmad today? In an insane asylum somewhere? Or has he died? I doubt I will ever find out.

• • •

Another long night on the sea. Martin and I realized we had a serious problem to manage: our diarrhea. I thought to myself, *This situation is going to get very embarrassing.*

Would you believe that we traveled across the water all night long, and neither of us ever had to go?! By the time we got to the peninsula coast, daylight had come. As soon as we stepped onshore and found a log to hide behind, the need struck us both with full force. I believe that was just the Lord's goodness—a small shield from needless humiliation.

The night had its terrors, however, in that we were out on the open ocean in the darkness, and whenever another boat got close to ours, we had to crouch down and stay covered under a tarp. At one point, a government patrol boat, complete with cannons poking over the side, was spotted. My heart began to pound as I thought, *This is it. This is the end of us. In just a few minutes we're going to get blasted into the sea, and we'll drown.*

I pled with God to spare our lives. I found myself repeating one phrase over and over: "O God, save us! O God, save us! O God, save us!"

Our captain turned on one small light at the back that shone down into the water, thus pretending to be a fishing boat. His ruse worked, and the patrol boat passed by without investigating.

We soon learned that an older man aboard our boat named Mirsab, who was about fifty-six years old, knew the immediate area from his earlier days with the Moro Islamic Liberation Front. He became our guide.

Once we landed, we set up camp in the jungle once again. We hadn't been there long when a group of civilians arrived unannounced to talk to Musab. This was problematic, because they obviously saw the white faces of Martin and me; there was no chance to hide us. Who knew what this group would do with that information?

We promptly moved again, but the pattern kept repeating itself: discovery by civilians, another march to another place. Talk of negotiation and release faded; we were back to the same old grind as on Basilan, only in this case, it became apparent that the Abu Sayyaf didn't really know where they were going. Once we mobiled beyond the territory that Mirsab knew well, we just wandered aimlessly in the jungle.

At this time, Martin developed worse intestinal problems than ever before. His need to go into the woods was unceasing. He worried that at night he wouldn't be able to get someone to unchain him fast enough so he could go. Bless his heart, as a precaution he began wearing some of the rags we had brought from Island 11, almost like a diaper, just in case he had an accident. *Oh, what I wouldn't give for a single bottle of Pepto-Bismol or a few tablets of Imodium A-D to help him,* I thought. But there was none.

Meanwhile, we pleaded with the Great Physician for relief. And within a few days, the worst of it passed.

By now his weight loss was obvious to everyone, not just me as his wife. The Abu Sayyaf needed to keep him alive for obvious reasons, so his food budget was improved. He began to regain a little weight. At least his bones weren't protruding to the point that they were visible through his T-shirt.

We would look at each other and sigh. I remembered back to our early years of marriage, how we would romanticize, "Won't it be nice to grow old together someday?" Well, that was exactly what we were doing there in the jungle. Only we weren't in our seventies or eighties. We just looked like it. For a time, we weren't allowed to bathe in the river for fear of being discovered. We were so awful and messy from the diarrhea. I finally went to Sabaya one day and said, "I can't go on like this. I need to do laundry, at least. If you don't start treating us differently, you just may as well go ahead and shoot me."

Martin, of course, kept trying to get me to calm down and be less dramatic, but that is truly how I felt. He went to Sabaya and said, "You know, really, if you'll just let us get back to bathing and taking care of ourselves, we won't be so dejected. Our depression is coming from being so filthy."

This succeeded in getting us back to the water on almost a daily basis, but not during the daylight hours. We had to bathe at twilight or even after dark, when they thought civilians were probably elsewhere.

One day I said to Sabaya, "Remember that book about alms-giving that Musab loaned me a while back? I read something very interesting in that—in fact, I even memorized the page number.

"On page 65 it says that some people asked Muhammad one day, 'How can a man be closest to paradise and the furthest from hell?' Muhammad said, 'Free a slave or let a captive go.'

"What about this? That's how the Prophet, may his name be blessed forever, answered the question." I thought I was really being clever by using their verbiage.

Sabaya was not impressed or convinced. "Oh, he was talking about some Muslims who had taken other Muslims captive. That passage refers only to a Muslim-Muslim thing; it has nothing to do with you."

So much for my efforts at theological persuasion.

But Martin wasn't making a lot of headway, either. One time

Sabaya confided that he missed his wives. He said he also missed Angie, his "booty of war." That led to a discussion of American courtship.

"We try to teach our sons the biblical standard of staying pure until marriage," Martin explained. "I wish I could be home teaching that to my teenage son right now, in fact. Boys need to learn to be responsible when dating."

"Well, men think about women all the time," Sabaya countered. "It's just ridiculous to think a man would restrain himself. 'Boys will be boys,' you know. But if a girl sleeps with someone before marriage, she is to be put to death. Or at best, she is only good enough to be a slave the rest of her life. That's just the rules." The blatant injustice of this setup apparently didn't cross his mind.

• • •

Days dragged on. We heard Sabaya on the satellite phone threatening to take matters into his own hands if the intermediary didn't start producing results. Where were the other 30 million pesos? he demanded.

What neither he nor we knew was that among the American advisers, the tide had turned against making further payments. Their intelligence seemed to indicate that the first money had only produced squabbling within the Abu Sayyaf. The conclusion was that to pay more would simply be throwing good money after bad.

Finally, Musab decided to go to the city and take charge. This would also give him a chance to see his family again, which was a priority for him. We got our hopes up once more; after all, Musab was the second-in-command of the whole organization.

He said he would be gone only a few days. Time passed, and we all waited. Musab didn't return.

We kept waiting.

In fact, he never returned. Sabaya was furious. "Here Musab was always our preacher," he complained. "He was the one to

get us together on Fridays and tell us we all needed to be tough and endure hard things in our struggle for Allah. And now he abandons us!"

Every once in a while, Musab called on the sat-phone to talk to Ediborah. "I'm going to send for you this coming Friday," he would promise. She would get all ready to leave, parceling out her stuff to others. I would get her deodorant, perfume, and soap.

"Ediborah, why don't you just keep these until you actually leave?" I would say.

"No, no—he's promised me a boat is coming this Friday."

The day would pass, and no boat would show up. I would give her back her belongings. Others, however, did not; she ended up losing a long-sleeved shirt, among other things.

Obviously, Musab was not going to play the liberator role for either her or us.

Martin and I were journaling nearly every day. The Abu Sayyaf had even started ordering pens and paper when they saw us writing so often. Martin's journal entries pretty much convey the mood:

April 25, Thursday
It's hard to feel like something is really going to happen even though they say it will. We've been promised before. Sometimes it's as though we're just being strung along. There is nothing else to do but just keep going. . . . The Lord is faithful, and he is our strength.

April 26, Friday
The boat didn't come last night, so no new treats (or anything). There was the usual Friday [Abu Sayyaf] meeting that turned into a surprise when one of the members was taken into custody for expressing some form of dissent. Not sure

---

April 24
Another family statement of encouragement airs on Radyo Agong but is not heard by Martin and Gracia.

what his fate will be. . . . One of the guys came running at me with his gun and a rope. I thought maybe things were over, but they [only] wanted my handcuffs for the new prisoner who has been declared more dangerous than I. First time I've had the cuffs completely off since I don't remember when. Feels kind of funny. It's like I forgot to get dressed or put on my watch.

We're still waiting for news. No idea what will happen.

April 27, Saturday

Who would have thought we'd still be here after 11 mos.? It just keeps going on. The boat didn't come again last night—engine trouble again. I was not chained last night because they're chaining their member. Good thing, as I had bad LBM. Many trips up the mountain. Not too much sleep for me as I didn't trust myself.

April 28, Sunday

The boat arrived finally last night. More rice and reinforcements, although 2 did go out. My "personal" was new handcuffs. Just what I wanted! . . .

Sabaya did a radio interview. He denies that our ransom has been paid. We'll have to see what the story is when we get out. I still believe it will happen. Just don't know when. Maybe next week.

In a letter to the kids at this same time, which was written but never dispatched, Martin wrote:

Jeff, are you driving yet? I have been wondering. If we take a family vacation you can help with the driving now. That should be strange.

We have been trying to imagine life outside for some time now. We wear the same clothes all the time. They're like pajamas. . . . Someone gave me a button shirt and that has been nice.

. . . We will never get back this lost year, but hopefully we will all be stronger for it. Your mother has had a hard time with all this—more than I, I suppose. She just wants a friend. I need to keep trying, and we all need to be supportive of her. She still thinks sometimes that this is her fault because she made the plans for Dos Palmas. God has much to teach us about forgiveness, but the place to begin is forgiving ourselves. This is the fault of the Abu Sayyaf, and no one else.

God has a purpose. I will never understand why he has allowed it to go on so long. Guess we still have need of patience. I will say that my faith has been strengthened. I think your mother's has as well. We do struggle, though.

Love, Dad

19

ONE RAINY AFTERNOON

(May–Early June 2002)

With each move, we seemed to be heading inland into the higher, more remote elevations of the Zamboanga Peninsula. We knew this was not good because it portended more hiding out and a continued stalemate.

At least the Abu Sayyaf had new phones, thanks to the ransom money, which allowed us to order supplies. One day when Alvin Siglos asked what we wanted, I said, "How about some new boots for me?"

He did try to get the boots, but every time a new pair arrived in camp, they were pilfered by others who wanted boots, too. Finally, on the sixth try, I got my boots.

Since the money was still available, we decided to ask Alvin for a Scrabble game. We were looking forward to some friendly competition to keep our minds sharp. I heard later that three or four Scrabble sets had been bought, but none of them ever reached us.

At times, we were forced to hike on terrain that was so steep we could hardly keep our footing without hanging on to a tree. Once on a steep hill, I dislodged a rock that rolled down and hit Martin's leg. He limped for the rest of the day, and I felt horrible about that.

One night when the guys went down to wait for the *banca* that

would be carrying our supplies, a boat pulled up and started to unload. Our guys went out to greet them with the usual *"Salam alaikom!* [Peace to you!]"—only to discover that these were AFP troops! We hadn't seen the armed forces for weeks, ever since leaving Basilan. Now they were back on our trail.

The guys took off running in a panic and managed to get away. But the soldiers had obviously seen them and could no doubt follow their footprints. We wondered if they'd be able to find us, and so we spent the next days on alert.

In this area were lots of *kalaw,* or duckbills—beautiful, big birds with bright red bills. Since we couldn't go to town for food now, the Abu Sayyaf shot several *kalaw* for us to eat.

On a bright Sunday morning, some of the guys began building cooking fires so we could prepare the *kalaw.* But suddenly, a hand was raised and we all got silent. One of the guys thought he had heard something down the hill. We quickly began to pack up our stuff. Mirsab, the guide, spotted soldiers heading up the hill and again motioned for us to be silent. My heart began to pound loudly. I never did get used to these confrontations.

All of a sudden, shots were fired from one side of the ridge. Ediborah began running down the other side.

I thought back to a conversation she and I had had a few days earlier.

"What if this negotiation doesn't go through?" she had asked. "What if we're here for a long, long, long time? Can we keep doing this?"

"We have to," I replied. "We don't have any other options. Are you thinking we should try to escape?"

"No. I'm just asking if we're strong enough mentally and physically to keep on." Now that she was alone, without Musab, she seemed so much more vulnerable.

Later we learned that Musab was trying to get one million pesos ($20,000) from a Manila senator for her release, but the senator kept stalling. This made Sabaya look bad, since he had announced

over the radio that Ediborah would soon be released as an act of good faith on the Abu Sayyaf's part. Now he couldn't make good on his promise, thanks to Musab's wheeling and dealing.

I watched as Ediborah ran off, and I decided to follow her.

"Stop!" Martin called after us. "You need to stay here! We'll get in trouble." But we kept running.

Along the trail, I slid in the mud, scratching up my arm and wrenching my back. Martin stayed behind Ediborah and me, following us closely. Finally we reached the river, where we hid behind a rock overhang. I expected that the Abu Sayyaf would withdraw here as well and we'd all head upriver. I had assumed wrong.

"Hey, Martin!" came a call from high on the ridge. "Get back up here! Where's Gracia? Where's Ediborah?"

"We're all here," he called out. "Don't shoot at us!"

We had to climb back up the hill, and by the time the three of us reached the top, we were spent. Nevertheless, we joined the rest in mobiling along the ridge. It proved to be a hard trek.

When we finally stopped for a rest, Sabaya confronted Martin. "Why did you run?!"

"I ran because the ladies ran."

I figured I'd better speak up, too. "I ran because Ediborah ran."

"Were you trying to escape?"

"No, honestly," Martin replied. "I was just concerned about the women."

Sabaya's eyes narrowed as he said, "If you ever run again, I will shoot you." Turning to his comrades, he added, "If he ever runs again, you shoot him."

Everyone got quiet then, and from that point on, security was definitely tighter. After nearly a year in the jungle, Martin's bravery and optimism finally began to crack. He wrote:

May 6, Monday
Slept on the ground. I'm so discouraged. Usually I'm not, but

today I am. PTL [praise the Lord] for Gracia. She's saying all "my" lines [of encouragement] and I'm thinking all "her" thoughts from the past. Only dif[ference] is (I guess) I'm too dumb to stop, but I really feel like I'm going to die here. I think the ladies will get out because it's the "right" thing, but not me. . . . We're going to walk and walk. God, please give us strength for the journey.

If I was any encouragement to Martin, it was more through the songs I sang rather than anything I may have said. I would go through the alphabet trying to sing a song whose title began with each letter: "Abide with Me," "Blessed Assurance," "Calvary Covers It All," etc. One morning as the sun came up, I rolled out of the hammock to give him more room and sat on a sack of rice, singing songs for the occasion:

"When Morning Gilds the Skies"
"Precious Lord, Take My Hand"
"Reach Out to Jesus"
"When We All Get to Heaven"

Among the most uplifting songs was "His Strength Is Perfect" by Steven Curtis Chapman, which begins, "His strength is perfect when our strength is gone."

I modified the words for a second and third chorus: "His will is perfect" and "His way is perfect."

I had to sing quietly for two reasons: The Abu Sayyaf didn't think singing was appropriate (although they had tolerated it in the past) and none of us wanted to be discovered by the AFP. So my singing voice, which in the past had been trained to project well, became

---

May 7
A two-page article in *People* magazine features the Burnham plight.

---

quiet and quavery. *Will I ever get to cut loose and sing strongly again?*
I wondered.

Assad had been wounded the day that we had run from the
soldiers, but he was still able to walk. Good thing, because for a
week or so, we hiked and hiked. Our captors had a destination in
mind, they said, and when we got to that village, they would release
us to the barrio captain. *Oh, really?* I thought. *I'll believe that when
I see it.*

Meanwhile, food was harder to get here on the peninsula because
it wasn't a farming area. It was more given to logging. Whereas on
Basilan we always knew that bananas and coconuts were nearby, here
we were at the mercy of the *banca* deliveries. What this region lacked
in food supply, however, it more than made up for in mosquitoes.
They were ferocious.

We pressed on with difficult hiking, not sure where this village
really was. Occasionally a guy was sent to climb a tree and look for
it amid the sea of green. We mainly wandered through the forest.

Rumors abounded. Supposedly Malaysia was still going to pay
a ransom for us.

On May 20, Martin got up the nerve to ask to borrow Sabaya's
shortwave radio. Searching the dial for Voice of America to get the
news, he happened upon KNLS, a Christian station out of Alaska.
A short devotional came on, only two or three minutes. The pastor,
named Andy Baker, read from Romans 8:

> *If God is for us, who can be against us? He who did not spare
> his own Son, but gave him up for us all—how will he not also,
> along with him, graciously give us all things? Who will bring
> any charge against those whom God has chosen? It is God who
> justifies. Who is he that condemns? Christ Jesus, who died—
> more than that, who was raised to life—is at the right hand of
> God and is also interceding for us. (vv. 31-34)*

What an amazing selection—the first spoken Scripture we had heard in almost a year.

"If you are in the midst of a hard situation," Pastor Baker said, "and if you could hear Christ in the next room praying, you wouldn't be afraid of thousands of enemies. He would be calling your name."

Martin and I looked at each other with tears in our eyes. The speaker then began to lead in prayer—for people who were oppressed, people on the West Bank and in Afghanistan, and people who were being treated wrongly because of their faith in Christ. It seemed like he was praying for us. We were overwhelmed.

• • •

One of the many target dates we had set in our minds for release was Saturday, May 25. We knew from a letter received long ago that my niece Sally would be married that day in Indianapolis, the first of my nieces to be wed. All the family would be gathered for the festive occasion. Earlier, we had hoped to be there as well, of course.

Instead, we passed this day in the jungle, praying repeatedly for Sally and Tom, that God would bless their new life together. We tried to imagine what all was happening. We knew that this was the last marker on our mental calendar; we had now run out of information about what anyone was doing back home.

The next Monday, May 27, marked our one-year anniversary of captivity. The day came—and went. Long ago, we would never have believed we'd be in captivity this long. But there we were.

May 27
To mark the one-year anniversary of captivity, Radyo Agong plays an appeal for release from Martin's parents.

May 28
A candlelight prayer service is held in front of the U.S. embassy in Manila.

By now we had heard that several shiploads of soldiers had landed on the Zamboanga Peninsula. It was clear that the noose was tightening around us.

One day while walking along, the leader of our group suddenly ducked down. Not knowing what was ahead, the rest of us ducked as well. Across the next hill, we spotted two soldiers eating their lunch, talking and laughing. From the conversation, it sounded like other buddies of theirs would be coming along soon. We quickly changed course.

With this change in direction, our supply line had been cut entirely. We were on our own to find food and even water. Life got very hard, harder than it had been our entire time in captivity. The hiking was tough as we tried to stay high in the mountains; the soldiers seemed to prefer the lowlands. Struggling along the trail with the heavy pack on my back, I silently recited from Hebrews 12:1-2 (KJV):

> *Wherefore seeing we also are compassed about with so great*
> *a cloud of witnesses, let us lay aside every weight, and the sin*
> *which doth so easily beset us, and let us run with patience the*
> *race that is set before us, looking unto Jesus the author and*
> *finisher of our faith; who for the joy that was set before him*
> *endured the cross, despising the shame, and is set down at the*
> *right hand of the throne of God.*

We were still carrying some rice, but we'd lost our cooking pots that Sunday morning when the *kalaw* meal got interrupted. Everyone was hungry. (Sabaya, in the same battle, had lost his cherished Colt .45 pistol. I silently rejoiced, because all along, I had figured he would use that to finish us off if he got into some desperate spot.)

Martin remembered that a year before, our son Jeff had gone on a survival week sponsored by Faith Academy. He had come home telling us how to cook rice in bamboo. We could take a section, he

told us, drill a hole in the side, fill it with rice and water, then heat the bamboo over the fire.

Martin explained this to the guys. We got to a river where some bamboo was growing, but they were reluctant to try it because soldiers were all around and chopping down bamboo can get noisy. In the end, however, hunger overruled caution, and soon we had something to eat. Martin and I had to smile at this turn of events, thanks to the insights of our son now so many thousands of miles away.

However, at other times there was no bamboo available. We eventually came down to just our remaining salt and raw rice. When we couldn't stand the hunger anymore, we resorted to chewing on the raw rice. It was supposed to be group food, but I confess I ignored the rules and helped myself more than once. I had adopted the excuse "If I need it, it's not really stealing" at last.

Some of the boys ate so much that Sabaya grew worried about the dwindling supply. He gathered up everyone's remaining stock and committed it to Martin to carry—the only person he could trust not to devour it. This meant Martin wound up with an even heavier load than before.

After several days, the leaders announced that we would have an easier time hiking on the logging roads than the trails. That concerned me; it meant that the chances of being discovered by a logger or other civilian were much higher. I voiced my reservations but was overruled.

We set out in the morning. Suddenly the two men at the head of the line wheeled around and came running back in our direction. *"Sundalo! Sundalo!"* We all turned around and began to run the opposite direction.

The soldiers must have had radios to communicate with each other, because off in the distance, we heard trucks start up the mountain, heading our way. We darted off the road, scrambling over the piles of leftover branches and brush, called "slash." This wasn't a fast process, of course. As we began climbing the

mountainside, my heart was racing from both the exertion and the danger, but I didn't dare stop.

By this time, Ediborah had lost her shoes and was walking barefoot. We ended up walking the rest of the day.

We were still in search of the village where, allegedly, more ransom would be paid, and then all would be well. That evening we came to another logging road. We sat in the forest waiting for the cover of darkness, then got organized to dash across, three at a time.

When it was Martin's and my turn, we made our run, along with a guard named Sarin. In the middle of the road, I glanced up—and there was a civilian coming right toward us! I couldn't believe it.

A commotion followed as the Abu Sayyaf took this fellow hostage; they couldn't afford to just let him keep walking down the road. I felt so sorry for him, especially when he was chained to a tree for the night. As I lay down to sleep, I could just imagine what was going through his mind: *Why did I have to come along at just that moment? How did I get into this mess? Will I ever get out alive?* It turned out that he worked for the logging company and knew the area much better than Mirsab did. This qualified him to be our guide up at the head of the line.

• • •

It had now been nine days since our last true meal. We were reduced to eating leaves. I would pick a leaf and ask the others whether or

---

May 29
The United States offers up to $5 million in reward money for information leading to the arrest of Janjalani, Musab, Sabaya, Solaiman, or Hamsiraji Sali, another of the captors.

June 3
The Burnham children head to Arkansas for a summer visit with Gracia's parents, her brother, and his family.

---

not it was safe to eat. We tried to keep drinking plenty of water that we gathered from rivers or collected when it rained.

As we hiked, we came to yet another logging road. Since it had been raining, we couldn't help but leave tracks in the mud. I appealed to Sarin again. "Is there any way you could talk to the guys and point out how dangerous it is to be on these roads?"

He ignored me. Again, we waited until dark to cross.

When I got to the other side, I misstepped and fell about three feet down into some of the slash. A couple of others did the same. As I worked my way back up, I scraped my back and wrenched my arm. Nevertheless, we kept walking, eventually crossing a river before we were allowed to stop, totally exhausted, around two or three in the morning.

There was no moon; it was an especially dark night. We couldn't see what we were doing. We put up our hammocks as best we could and lay down to rest.

I thought we would at least get to finish the night there. But an hour or so later, we were aroused to get moving again. "Dawn is coming soon, and we have to be out of here." We were groggy and disoriented as we fumbled around in the darkness for our belongings.

On the trail Ediborah said to me, "I felt really alone last night. Nobody helped me set up my hammock, and I couldn't find two trees that were close enough. I just had to sleep on the ground."

"Oh, Ediborah, I'm so sorry that happened," I told her. "You're really all alone, aren't you?"

"Yes. Actually, that wasn't the worst of it. I ended up on an anthill. I didn't sleep at all."

After the sun had come up, we ran into, of all things, a farm! It had nangka trees and marang and coconut. Soon we were all shoving this unripe fruit into our mouths as fast as we could and drinking the coconut milk. We gorged ourselves, then hit the road once again.

About eight that morning, we stopped to set up our hammocks.

Apparently our captors intended to spend the day in this place. Up on the hill, we could see the logging road we had crossed. A truck came along. It stopped at a point I calculated to be about where we had been during the night. We could hear voices talking excitedly, and then some shouting.

"Pack up! Pack up!" came the order. Soon we were on the move once again, up, down, up, down. We came to a couple more farms, then some swamps.

I remember saying to Martin that day for about the five hundredth time, "I just don't think I can keep doing this much longer. I can't take this anymore."

And he answered, like so often before, "You know, Gracia, I just think we're going to get out of here soon. I think this is all going to work out. After we're home, this is going to seem like such a short time to us. Let's just hold steady."

At about twelve or twelve-thirty we could see a rain front moving in. The Abu Sayyaf began looking for another place to stop. We crested a mountain and started down the other side toward a little stream. The slope was very steep—maybe as much as forty degrees. From top to bottom, its length was no more than a city block, with low vegetation covering it. We brought out our hammocks once again.

It was June 7. "You know, tomorrow is my brother Paul's birthday," I said as we worked to get the hammock set up.

"Oh, yeah, that's right," Martin replied, with a long look at me.

Neither of us said any more. We both knew what the other was thinking: *Wouldn't it be nice to be out for that, so we could give Paul a call?* But by now, there was no point in verbalizing such wishes. We let the matter drop.

We also put up our *tolda,* as it looked like the rain would start at any moment. Ediborah was having trouble again finding suitable trees.

"Can I help you?" Martin asked.

"No, I think I just found a place. I'll be okay." She was up the hill and a little to our right.

We sat in the hammock a minute. Martin was in a reflective mood. He said, "I really don't know why this has happened to us. I've been thinking a lot lately about Psalm 100—what it says about serving the Lord with gladness. This may not seem much like serving the Lord, but that's what we're doing, you know? We may not leave this jungle alive, but we can leave this world serving the Lord 'with gladness'; we can 'come before his presence with singing' [Psalm 100:2, KJV]."

We prayed together then, something we did often. There was nothing else to do; we were totally dependent upon the Lord. We thanked the Lord for bringing us this far safely, and of course we begged him to get us home and back to our kids. We told him we wanted to keep serving him with gladness.

Martin had a toenail that had become ingrown. He borrowed a knife from the guys nearby and worked on his nail for a while. It gave me the creeps to watch him. But he said it started to feel better.

We returned the knife to the guys and then decided to lie down for a nap. It was starting to rain. We had just closed our eyes when a fearsome barrage of gunfire cut loose from the crest of the hill. The AFP? Surely not! It was raining, and they never fought in the rain.

"Oh, God!" I said. I wasn't swearing; I was honestly praying. My instincts, after sixteen previous battles, told me instantly what to do: *drop immediately.* I flipped my feet around to get out of the hammock—and before I even hit the ground, I felt the *zing!* of a bullet slamming through my right leg.

I rolled down the steep hill maybe eight feet, dazed. I looked up and saw Martin on the ground, too, so I quickly crawled to his side. He was kind of twisted, with his legs underneath his body. His eyes were closed. He was wearing a white Suzuki shirt with blue sleeves. Then I saw it: the blood was beginning to soak through his shirt from his upper left chest. *Oh no!* I thought. *He's been hit, too.*

Shots continued to ring out. The Abu Sayyaf were just getting

themselves positioned to start firing back. Martin's breathing was heavy, almost a soft snore. He lay quietly on his back and partly on his side; he was so still that I refrained from yelling about my wound, which is what I normally would have done.

"Mart!" I heard Ediborah yell from where she was, just one time. Then nothing more. It was the last word she ever said.

I thought to myself, *If the Abu Sayyaf see that I'm wounded but still alive, they'll drag me down the hill, and I'll have to walk while wounded.* So I deliberately tried to lie still and look dead. Martin had taught me to focus my mind in a firefight, to hang on tightly to my emotions, and I knew that now, more than ever, I needed to do just that.

Once in a while, he moaned softly. I didn't say anything to him but just focused on being still. The shooting continued. Grenades blew up. Each moment was going to be my last, I was sure. *Lord, if this is it, just make it happen quickly for me,* I prayed. The battle raged. The pain in my leg was not as severe as the terror in my heart. I forced myself to keep lying still.

Several minutes passed. Then without warning I felt Martin's body become heavy and sort of sag against mine.

Is he dead? I wondered. I had no experience by which to judge. *Maybe he just passed out.*

The shooting gradually became more sporadic and then finally stopped. At the top of the ridge I heard shouting in Tagalog, the language of the AFP. No sounds came from the bottom, however, which told me that the Abu Sayyaf had fled down the streambed.

I didn't want to startle anyone who might be nearby, so I slowly moved my hand to signal that I was still alive. Immediately an AFP soldier spotted me. He and his partner ran down and tried to pick me up, one by lifting my shoulders, the other my ankles. I cried out in pain. So they let me down again, and both took a shoulder to pull me back toward our hammock and *tolda*. In the wetness they couldn't get a good grip on me, and their feet were slipping as well.

I looked back at where Martin still lay. The red spot on his shirt was larger now. His complexion was pasty white. And then I knew—the man I loved more than anyone in the world was gone.

• • •

I wanted to stop the world in that moment, to reflect on my dreadful loss, to mourn the senseless death of my wonderful husband. Unfortunately, circumstances demanded otherwise. I had to think about getting myself off this mountain alive.

I gazed upward at our *tolda.* It had been riddled with bullet holes. As we had feared for so long, the AFP had come upon us with all barrels blazing.

"Did you get Sabaya?" I asked.

"Yeah, we think so. The one with the long hair?"

"No—that's Lukman. Sabaya was under the green *tolda* over there. Check that one."

A search revealed that he had gotten away.

The soldiers yelled up the slope for more help in moving me. Somehow we reached the top of the hill.

There I remembered the green backpack. It was still back by our hammock and it had all the notes we had written, the letters to the children, the stories. "Go get that green bag," I said. "I've got to have that."

The soldiers looked at me like I was crazy.

"Go get that green bag!" I insisted. "It has letters from Martin to our children. It will be the only thing they have left from their dad. You have to get it!"

One of the soldiers said to me, "Oh, Martin's okay. . . ."

I stared back at him. "Martin is *dead.* All the kids are going to have left is what he's written to them in the green bag. *Please* go get it!"

At that, one of them disappeared over the ridge. In a minute, he

came back with the precious bag. I reached out to touch it, but they wouldn't let me. "We have to go over it for intelligence," someone said, which I thought was ridiculous.

There was some arguing about when I would get the papers inside. I locked eyes with one soldier whose English was pretty good. "Do you swear you'll get those letters to me?"

"Yes, ma'am, I will."

By this time, the medic was starting to cut off my wet *pantos*. I leaned back to close my eyes. Suddenly I was so exhausted, I just wanted to close my eyes and drift off into sleep.

"Oh, no, don't go to sleep," I heard someone say. "Stay awake."

The medic looked at me with a big smile and announced in heavily accented English, "I am the medic, and you are my first patient!" His hands were shaking. He proceeded to wrap some cloth around my wounds and then pronounced cheerfully, "Okay, you're all right! Do you need anything else?"

I stared blankly at him. "Do you have a Tylenol?" I asked him.

"Sure, okay." He didn't even have medicine with him, so he began asking around. Somebody came up with some mefenamic acid, an anti-inflammatory drug, which I took.

Somebody else brought dry clothes for me. Soon I was told, "A helicopter is coming for you."

I looked up at the rain still coming down. "A helicopter can't come right now," I said. "The ridges aren't clear, and it's raining."

They looked at me as if to say, *What do you know, lady?* They didn't realize I was a pilot's wife who had tracked the weather for hundreds of flights in my life. I knew it wasn't safe for a helicopter to operate under these conditions.

"No, no, for you the helicopter will come," someone answered.

"No! Please don't call one," I pleaded. "The pilot can't see what he's doing, and I don't want anyone else to lose their life today. Let's just wait." Nevertheless, the helicopter was already on its way.

The soldiers were clearly upset, realizing that in their rescue

attempt, they had shot all three hostages. Several of them were smoking to calm their nerves. *I can't go to sleep, and I can't fall apart here,* I told myself. *I've made it this far.* I tried to remember Martin's words from so many times before: "You can do this, Gracia. You've got to go home whole."

Eventually, the lieutenant in charge came over to talk with me.

"Mrs. Burnham, I know that you're probably very angry with us," he said. "But we were just doing our jobs."

"I know," I replied. "We never forgot who the bad guys were and who the good guys were. I don't think of you as the bad guys."

In a moment, I continued. "How did you find us?"

"We've been following you all day. We saw your tracks where you crossed the logging road last night."

I knew it! We hadn't been careful enough.

I told them how hungry we were after so many days without food.

"Yeah, we saw where you ate your breakfast this morning at the farm. We just kept tracking you."

A little later, I heard the *chop-chop-chop* of a helicopter rotor. The ridges had cleared, and a little patch of blue was starting to peek through the clouds. "Now close your eyes, because it's going to be very windy," someone said. "We don't want you to get anything in your eyes."

Soon they were carrying me in a *malong* to the floor of the chopper. There I opened my eyes. I looked at the pilot, hoping he was an American, but I couldn't tell. Several of the soldiers wounded in the battle were already sitting on the seats. They strapped me down and closed the door.

But wait! What about Martin's body? Was I just going to be whisked away and leave my husband on this soggy hillside? *This can't be. . . .* I leaned back and sadly realized that in my physical condition, I had no other choice. We pulled away into the sky, leaving my best friend lying in the rain.

20
THE EMBASSY
(June 7–10, 2002)

IN LESS THAN THIRTY MINUTES, the Black Hawk set down at an airport in Zamboanga City, and my world instantly changed from rugged jungle to paved runways, modern terminal buildings, electricity, running water, toilets with privacy, professional-looking signs—it almost made my head spin. The helicopter door slid back, and immediately I saw American troops. An ambulance was waiting with an honest-to-goodness stretcher. Within minutes I was on a bumpy road heading for Camp Navarro General Hospital, which had been set up several months before to serve the U.S. military advisers and other staff.

When we arrived at the hospital and the ambulance door opened again, I was suddenly surrounded by people, everyone talking all at once. In the distance I noticed a beautiful American servicewoman. Her dark hair was pulled back and she was dressed in fatigues. She smiled at me, and I smiled back. As medics whisked me into the facility, I saw a whole row of U.S. troops with automatic rifles standing guard. The guys seemed so huge! After 376 days of living with short Filipinos, I was struck by their size. I began to realize that all this security was just for me.

Once in the examining room, the doctors moved in, one after another. All kinds of activity swirled around me. The American servicewoman never left the foot of my bed. When things grew

calm for a moment, she introduced herself: "I'm Major Reika Stroh. I'm going to stay with you until you don't need me anymore." She began to stroke my arm and play with my fingers. I lay back and thought how nice it felt.

Who had planned ahead to provide this special service? I wondered.

Soon I was ushered into X-ray. Once again, I glanced sideways to see the security detail still standing guard. The attention was almost overwhelming.

The X-rays found that no bones had been chipped or broken and no arteries had been hit by the bullet; it had passed through the flesh from the back of my thigh out the front. I needed surgery to close the two wounds, but it was a simple enough procedure that it could be done right away at this facility.

They gave me a shot of anesthesia; I closed my eyes and drifted into unconsciousness.

When I awoke, it was dark. Major Stroh told me that although the surgery had gone well, some shrapnel had to be left behind. My leg wasn't in a cast, but a thick wrapping engulfed it from near my hip down to my knee.

I was well enough to leave and the American authorities wanted to fly me to Manila, she explained. "The whole mission of this plane and its crew has been to sit on the tarmac and wait for you and Martin to come out of the jungle," she told me. "They'll finally get to finish their mission."

Once we got back to the airfield and my stretcher was safely clipped to the wall of the huge C-130, Major Stroh said, "General

---

June 7
3:00 A.M.: The phone rings in Kansas. U.S. Ambassador to the Philippines Francis Ricciardone tells Paul and Oreta that their son is dead and their daughter-in-law is wounded.

June 7
3:30 A.M.: President Arroyo calls the Burnhams to confirm the news.

[Donald] Wurster is here to meet you." I had seen a picture of this U.S. Air Force brigadier general in a *Newsweek* magazine while we were in the jungle, so I knew that he was the commander of the joint task force in the southern Philippines. I wasn't alert enough to grasp everything he said, but he told me that he was glad I was finally out, and that I was going to be okay. He said something about my being brave and then added, "Here, I want you to have something."

He pressed the general's star from his cap into my hand.

"Oh, thank you very much," I said, overwhelmed with his thoughtfulness.

As soon as he left, I turned the star over to Major Stroh for safekeeping. "Are you hungry?" she asked. "We saved some of what we had for supper. Would you like some?"

Of course I did! But as soon as I took a bite, I began to feel nauseated. I realized that my stomach was simply not up to this yet.

The trip to Manila took less than an hour. There the U.S. ambassador, Francis Ricciardone, a distinguished-looking man in a suit, came onto the plane to say, "We are so glad you are here. Welcome to Manila. We're going to take you to the embassy." Within minutes I was in another ambulance headed through the nighttime streets of the capital.

Later I found out that, in order to protect me from the curious press, two decoy ambulances had already been sent toward Malacañang, the presidential palace. Meanwhile, we went the back way to the embassy and were there within ten or fifteen minutes. They had obviously planned all this in detail, and everything went like clockwork.

As we pulled through the security gates there on Roxas Boulevard, I gazed out at the palm trees and the beautifully manicured lawns and remembered when I had been to these buildings years before for passport matters. But this time, I saw rooms I'd never seen before. They wheeled me into a cozy two-bedroom suite with tasteful furniture and attractive art on the walls. There

was food in the refrigerator, and in the closet I found some of my own clothes, items the New Tribes people had brought down from Aritao months before in hopes that someday I'd be here to wear them.

Although it was late on a Friday night, Ted Allegra, the embassy's chief of American citizen services, was waiting for me. A wonderfully gracious man, he briefed me on everything that was going to happen, including a visit with President Arroyo. Then he asked me, "What are *your* wishes?"

"I want to get out of here as soon as possible. Or if I can't go home soon, I want my family to come and join me here."

"Your sister Mary is already on her way to escort you home. How about if we get you on your way by Monday morning?"

I was thrilled and told him so.

Ted then told me that he had called both my parents and Martin's, and that the AFP had managed to retrieve Martin's body from the hillside. "We're going to fly him to the big military hospital in Okinawa for an autopsy," he gently explained. I was relieved to know that he was finally in American hands.

"Is there anything else?" he asked.

I wondered if there was any way to contact Ediborah's children. "I know they don't live here in Manila, but I'm the only one who can tell them how their mother lived and died," I told him. "I'd also like the chance to talk with my coworkers from New Tribes Mission."

Ted looked at me a little oddly and said, "Well, I want you to know you are not a prisoner here at the embassy . . . but you may not leave."

I looked back and said, "Then I guess that means they'll all have to be invited here."

Ted sat there a minute and then said he'd try to make the arrangements.

When he left, I reached for the phone to call Martin's parents, having calculated that it would still be Friday morning in Kansas.

"Hello . . . this is Gracia, calling from Manila. I just wanted you to know that I'm fine."

"Hi, Gracia." I heard the voice of my mother-in-law on the other end of the line. "Doug is here with us, too." We talked for a minute and then I couldn't wait any longer.

"Can I talk to the kids?"

"They're not here—they've been with your folks in Arkansas for a few days, now that school has let out. Your brother and his family took everybody to the lake. But we've already been in touch with them, and they're driving back here to Kansas today."

I would have to wait just a bit longer to hear their voices. I was so disappointed.

But before we hung up, I knew I had to move ahead to the painful subject of Martin's death.

"I'm so sorry that Martin didn't make it out," I said to Oreta.

"We're sorry, too, but we're glad you're okay," she answered.

I proceeded to give them details of the last encounter, wanting them to hear it from me instead of the press. They were terribly sad, of course.

We talked about a tentative funeral date. Suddenly, I felt very tired. I looked at the clock and realized it was three-thirty in the morning! As we hung up, I promised I'd call again once I got some sleep.

A Filipino nurse arrived and cleaned me up a little bit. The feel of clean, warm water on my skin was such a soothing treat.

She gave me a bit of cranberry juice and helped me change into my pajamas. I looked at this bed, with its spotless sheets and comfortable mattress, and thought, *No hammock tonight! And no one is going to chain Martin ever again.*

I finally sank down and turned out the light, but rather than sleeping, I found myself reliving the scene of Martin's death.

June 7

4:30 A.M.: Mary Jones, having received a call during the night, passes the word to her parents in Arkansas, who must then tell the children.

I replayed in my mind those awful moments when we were both lying there wounded on the hillside in the rain. *What if I'd spoken to him and tried to wake him up? What if I'd rolled him over so the bleeding wouldn't have filled up his lungs so fast? Would he still be alive?*

I began to berate myself for not doing something, anything. But deep inside, I knew that no matter what I might have tried, the outcome would have been the same. Martin had lost massive amounts of blood and had been struggling to get his breath. Now he had gone directly into the Lord's presence . . . and I was left here in this nice bed in Manila—alone. This would be the first of an endless string of such nights to come.

Together we had imagined so many times what it would be like to be released and flown to Manila. We had talked about going to Mega Mall together, seeing our friends, going out to dinner, and celebrating. We certainly never wanted to imagine a scenario like this one.

I had just drifted off to sleep when sounds of gunfire erupted through the embassy. I quickly sat up in bed and began to scream. My heart was racing, but with my injured leg, I couldn't get out of bed to hit the floor.

The nurse came running.

"Who was shooting?" I demanded.

"There was no shooting," she assured me. "You're fine. Trust me—there was nothing."

She sat there with me until I got my bearings enough to realize my mind was playing tricks on me. I lay back down.

The next thing I knew, it was morning. I saw a Gideons Bible on the bed stand and I stretched over to pick it up.

What a privilege to hold this book in my hands once again! I turned on the lamp and opened to the Psalms. I began reading:

> *Deliver me from my enemies, O God;*
> *protect me from those who rise up against me.*
> *Deliver me from evildoers*
> *and save me from bloodthirsty men.*

See how they lie in wait for me!
  Fierce men conspire against me
  for no offense or sin of mine, O LORD. . . .
But I will sing of your strength,
  in the morning I will sing of your love;
for you are my fortress,
  my refuge in times of trouble.
O my Strength, I sing praise to you;
  you, O God, are my fortress, my loving God.
(Psalm 59:1-3, 16-17)

Soon the nurse was at the door. "What are you doing? It's only 6 A.M."

"I found this Bible here, and I'm reading it."

"Don't you think you ought to get some more sleep? You went to bed awfully late."

So to make her happy, I turned the light off and lay back down. After a few minutes of not sleeping, though, I turned the light back on and kept reading, this time from my favorite passage:

Therefore, since through God's mercy we have this ministry, we do not lose heart. . . . For God, who said, "Let light shine out of darkness," made his light shine in our hearts to give us the light of the knowledge of the glory of God in the face of Christ.

But we have this treasure in jars of clay to show that this all-surpassing power is from God and not from us. We are hard pressed on every side, but not crushed; perplexed, but not in despair; persecuted, but not abandoned; struck down, but not destroyed. . . .

Therefore we do not lose heart. Though outwardly we are wasting away, yet inwardly we are being renewed day by day. For our light and momentary troubles are achieving for us an eternal glory that far outweighs them all. (2 Corinthians 4:1, 6-9, 16-17)

I then began to pray. *Oh, Lord, thank you so much for my getting out . . . and that my leg is going to be okay. Thank you for the joy of having your Word in my hands once again. Please go with me through these next difficult days, and make my life a blessing.*

• • •

After breakfast, I was desperate to get back on the phone and try to reach my kids, but Ted Allegra told me it was too early—that they might not yet have arrived in Rose Hill from Arkansas. Meanwhile, he had a whole list of people who needed to see me that day: the ambassador, the doctor, even President Arroyo, who was scheduled to come around nine in the morning. I could see the staff already cleaning up the place for her arrival.

But as the morning wore on, we learned that President Arroyo's trip had been delayed and that she wouldn't arrive until evening.

"Then let's try to call my kids," I said. A speakerphone was provided, and I eagerly dialed the number. I knew it would be about nine o'clock Friday evening in Kansas.

"Hi, everybody—it's Gracia!"

The room was full: Paul and Oreta, my mom and dad, Martin's brother Doug and his family, his youngest sister, Felicia, and her husband—and Jeff, Mindy, and Zach.

"Mom, you ought to see our front yard!" Jeff said.

"Why?"

"There's news media all over! Television cameras and everything. I even called the cops on some of them when they got too pushy."

"Wow, that's amazing," I replied. "Hey, who else is there with you?" Others chimed in. "How are you feeling?" someone asked.

"Well, I'm here in the American Embassy in Manila, and actually I'm feeling okay. They did surgery on my leg yesterday afternoon down in Zamboanga, and it went pretty smoothly."

"When are you coming home?"

"How does Monday morning sound? Soon enough?" I kept

talking, trying to update them on the travel plans I'd made with Ted Allegra.

I hated to break the upbeat mood of the conversation, but I knew I needed to talk to the kids about their dad. I had read somewhere that when a loved one passes away, people want to know the details of exactly what happened, even if it's hard to hear. Like with Martin's parents, I wanted my children to hear it all from me, not from someone else. I asked if they were ready to hear about how their dad had died.

"Yeah, Mom, go ahead and tell us." So I plunged into the story. The rawness of the event was impossible to gloss over, of course.

I could hear sniffling on the other end of the line. I knew they were crying—this wasn't easy for anyone. When I finished the story, Felicia and several others left the room.

"Mom, are you going to have a nervous breakdown?" Mindy asked. "Everyone is expecting one."

"Oh, honey," I said, "I had my breakdowns in the jungle. Actually, I wasn't very strong there. But your dad sure was. I learned so much from him this past year."

Then she asked, "Are you going to make us move from here?"

Up to that point, I hadn't really thought about our next step. But I could tell from Mindy's tone that moving would not be popular. If my kids wanted to stay in Kansas, that's what we'd do.

"No, we'll live there," I said. "I'm not going to make you pull up and move again. We've been through some hard times, and we are really going to be a family again. From now on, we'll make our decisions together."

After I spoke with the kids, I had the chance to talk to others in the room. In her classic southern "Missourah" drawl, my mom said, "We are thrilled to hear from you, Gracia. We are happy and very sad at the same time, but it's so nice to hear your voice."

My dad, ever protective, jumped in to say, "Gracia, you're probably very tired now and need to stop talking." I told him no, that on the contrary I just wanted to talk and talk.

The kids seemed to feel the same way. As Zach excitedly told me about throwing Aunt Beth off the jet ski at the lake the day before, the other kids cut in to say what a wild driver he was!

At the same time, I kept hearing my folks repeat, "It's so good to hear your voice." They were afraid, I guess, that I would be too broken up to carry on a conversation. Instead, we were reconnecting in a wonderful way.

In retrospect, I think the phone call was especially bittersweet for Martin's family. I know they were glad I was alive, but at the same time they were also grieving the loss of their son and brother. It had to be extremely difficult for them. As for my kids, I think it simply helped to hear that I was okay.

That went well, I thought as we hung up. I was encouraged by their resiliency. Maybe what I'd said about rebuilding our lives as a family could be true after all.

As the day wore on, my room filled with a steady stream of visitors. One conversation ran into another, it seemed. I received several phone calls about Martin's body. The autopsy had been finished, and they wondered if they should leave his beard as it was or shave it off. I had no idea what to say. After several phone calls to his parents in the U.S., we decided to leave his beard on. He was so thin by the time he died, and I didn't want to scare the kids. I thought with his beard gone, it would just show how sunken his cheeks had become. I still don't know if I made the right decision there, because the kids had never seen him with such a long beard.

I spent the rest of the day meeting people, answering questions, and making decisions. At one point Major Stroh came to sit on the bed beside me and start the first of many debriefing sessions for intelligence purposes. I talked on and on about what life had been like the past year, how the Abu Sayyaf had treated us, and the various emotional peaks and valleys we'd been through. She diligently took notes on a pad, but when I got to the part about Martin discovering his handcuffs no longer worked, I suddenly lost control.

"No!" I yelled. "You can't write that down! It'll make him look

bad. He was so afraid people would think he was a chicken or something for not trying to escape! Don't tell anybody what I just said!" I was shrieking as I began to sob.

She put down her pen instantly and just sat quietly. Tears began to fill her eyes, too. She reached over to give me a big hug. We wept together, until finally I could calm down and regain my composure. I apologized for yelling at her, and we continued.

Later that afternoon, a State Department counselor arrived. Gary Percival specialized in hostage situations and was a really neat Christian guy. "You're going to get hit with a lot of press and a lot of people wanting you to do things you don't want to do," he told me. "You're also going to have to deal with people who love you and haven't been able to do anything for you for a year but wished they could. Now will be their big opportunity—whether you want what they have in mind or not. They won't consciously mean to run your life, but that's what it will amount to.

"You are going to have to decide how much you want to do, what you want to do, what you can let others do for you, and how to say no nicely to the rest." I hadn't thought about any of this, but I was grateful for the advice.

We talked for a long time. When I became teary-eyed as I shared parts of my story, he just sat there—unlike everyone else, who always ran to get me a tissue. Finally, Gary commented, "Do you notice I'm not getting up and getting anything for you?"

"Well, I hadn't really noticed."

"I'm going to let you ask for what you need. If you need a Kleenex, you can ask me for a Kleenex," he said. "You haven't had to make very many decisions for more than a year, and now you may not know how. I'll help you if you need help. But you have to express it."

I thought back to this advice more than once in the days and weeks ahead. The other thing Gary told me was, "It is not your job to make everybody happy now that you are out. Just from being with you for these few hours, I can tell that you want everything to

run smoothly, you want everybody to feel good, you don't want to disappoint anyone." This guy obviously had my number! "Your job now is not to make everybody happy with you. Your job is to do what is best for you and get on with your life.

"For example, you don't owe the media anything. Feel free to talk to them—in fact, it's probably good if you do. But don't feel like you're obligated to them. Just write out a good statement to make when you leave here, and another one for when you land in America, and you'll be set."

Later on, three of our mission leaders came to see me: Bob Meisel; Jody Crain, the field director; plus Macon Hare from the home office in the States. It was so good to see them and talk together.

Just before President Arroyo was set to arrive, it dawned on me that I hadn't yet prayed about the visit. In the jungle, Martin and I had prayed about every little thing. We had thanked God for every drink of water. Now here I was, only twenty-four hours into the midst of plenty, with a nice bed and medicine, and I could already see my whole attitude and thought process changing.

Martin's sister Cheryl, who lives in the Philippines, had come to be with me. I turned to her and said, "Would you sit down here and pray with me about President Arroyo's visit?" She held my hand and we prayed together. I can't tell you how good that felt.

President Arroyo finally showed up about nine that evening, complete with a video crew. I hadn't realized what a small person she was. I'm only five foot two, and she was noticeably shorter than I.

She was beautifully dressed. I knew she had had a long, hard day, and I was honored that she still came to see me so late. She brought a basket of orchids with other gorgeous flowers, as well as a basket of fruit. She sat on the couch near my chair, and at first, as the cameramen were maneuvering to get the angles they wanted, it seemed kind of awkward. She didn't quite know what to say, and neither did I.

"Tell me how you are feeling," she began.

"Fine—really, I'm doing very well," I answered. "My leg is going to be all right, they say."

What do I say now? I wondered.

Without thinking, I said the first thing that came to my mind. "You know, you might be interested in the fact that the Abu Sayyaf really don't like it that a woman is running this country, because they don't think much of women. Personally, it seems to me you're the first president who has ever said no to them. Maybe that's part of why they're upset that the Philippines would let a woman be president."

"No, I hadn't realized that," she said, keeping her composure.

I glanced over at Ted Allegra, who looked like he was about to have a heart attack.

Oops! That wasn't a very good way to start, was it?

I took a breath and said, "Um, would you like to hear about my husband, Martin, and how he died?"

"Yes, I would."

I began the story of our walking all night, getting to the hillside, setting up our hammocks, and then hearing gunfire start from the top of the hill. I went through it all. She was genuinely listening. By the end of the story, we were just sitting there facing each other and talking like two friends.

I told her I wasn't mad at anybody, and I wasn't blaming anybody—except the Abu Sayyaf. I assured her that we had never forgotten who the bad guys were.

Sometimes at night when I couldn't sleep in the jungle, I used to lie in the hammock and think of all the unkind things I would say to President Arroyo someday—about how her military was on the take, and how they were too proud to stand aside and let the Americans lead the rescue effort. I'd made up my little speech. It wasn't nice. My natural self wanted to blame someone.

Then I would try to tell myself either that it wasn't her fault, or that even if it was, she was responsible to God, not me, for her actions.

At this meeting, none of my venom came even close to the surface. I didn't feel like chewing her out after all. I knew the army felt very bad for what had happened. I didn't need to make anyone feel worse.

. . .

On Sunday, I fulfilled my wish and called my brother, Paul, to say happy birthday. We had a wonderful talk. He told me later, "When I first heard that Martin had been shot to death, I got very angry and bitter. But when I heard how well you were coping, something healed in my heart."

Around noon, my New Tribes Mission friends began to arrive—probably thirty of them altogether. Ted Allegra let them in six or eight at a time so I wouldn't be overwhelmed. What a special time we had, talking and crying and even laughing together. Everybody seemed to want to touch me and make sure I was okay.

Later in the day, I got a chance to meet Ediborah's four children, her mother, and her brother, all of whom President Arroyo had specially flown to Manila. We spent maybe an hour together, and I told them stories about the year and how brave Ediborah had been. I told them she had been a good cook and had even built the cooking fires when the guys were too lazy to do it. She had always looked good and smelled good. Her English had been excellent, I said, which was such a help in keeping us informed.

The family members were somber, of course, still grieving their loss. I did the best I could to comfort their hearts.

Of course, I was not about to leave the Philippines without a visit with my dear friends Angie and Fe. The girls had been waiting their turn for hours. They finally came walking through the door, cautiously at first, and then we fell into each other's arms for long, long hugs.

They looked so good! Beautiful haircuts, makeup, clothes that fit—we laughed about that. No more baggy clothes to hide our figures!

Buddy and Divine (Angie's brother-in-law and sister) were there, too. They told me about the injuries they'd sustained as we were escaping from the Lamitan hospital and about their recovery.

Angie and Fe got down on their knees beside my chair and we talked and talked. They told me someone had spotted Hurayra in the Zamboanga passport office, probably trying to head for Malaysia. That sharp-eyed person had tried to chase Hurayra but had lost him in the crowded street.

How good it was to see these girls I had come to love dearly, now smiling, talking, and rebuilding their lives. They had been through so much! We were survivors, and we celebrated until Ted announced that their time was up. He was afraid I was wearing down. But by now, I didn't want to be protected—I wanted to keep talking to my friends.

Later that evening, my sister Mary and her husband, Lance, arrived. What a thrill! She just came marching in and took over in her usual Mary way. She sat me down on the bed and then pulled out my wedding ring! She had ended up with it and hadn't yet given it to Mindy, in hope that I would someday be released. Mary had been saving it for me. I put it on as we sat there . . . my most prized possession!

Mary and I went through some of my stuff in the closet and figured out what I needed. The nurses had gone out to the market to buy some baggy pants that would fit over the fat dressing on my wound so I'd have something to wear home.

"Is there anything else I can do for you?" she asked.

"Well, how would you like to shave my legs? It's only been about four months now!"

"Sure!" So we headed for the bathtub. What a riot. As I recall, Mary, Cheryl, and two nurses all tried to help.

Mary was eager to update me on her pregnancy, now four months along. She told me she had been using my situation as a wonderful excuse. "Whenever I don't want to clean house or do the dishes, I tell Lance, 'Oh, I couldn't possibly do that—my sister is a hostage!'"

We talked late into the night as we packed up for the flight the next morning.

• • •

When we got to the airport early that Monday, the ambassador was there to greet me. Soon it was time for me to face the reporters.

I pulled out my notes, as Ted and Gary had advised, and made my statement.

> Good morning. Martin and I had so many dear friends here in the Philippines. You know who you are. Our friends in Malaybalay, in Brookes Point, in Darapida [our barrio in Aritao], in Manila—we love you so very much, and we thank you for the precious memories that you gave us during our fifteen years here. Martin loved this country with all his heart.
>
> We want to thank each and every one of you for every time you remembered us in prayer. We needed every single prayer you prayed for us during our ordeal in the jungle.
>
> We know there are countless of you who don't even know us who prayed and offered support also, and we thank you, too. We especially want to thank the military men, the Filipinos and the Americans, who risked and even gave their lives in order to rescue us. May God bless these men in their ongoing efforts.
>
> During our ordeal, we were repeatedly lied to by the Abu Sayyaf, and they are not men of honor. They should be treated as common criminals. We support all efforts of the government in bringing these men to justice.
>
> I return to the States this morning to rejoin my children and to put my life back together. Part of my heart will always stay with the Filipino people. Thank you.

And with that, I was wheeled into the Jetway for a Northwest Airlines flight to Tokyo, which would connect in Minneapolis with a flight bound for Kansas City. Looking out the window for my

last glimpse of the Philippines, I saw several dozen AFP soldiers enthusiastically waving good-bye to me from the tarmac. I knew I was closing the door on a sixteen-year era of my life. Everything was now about to change.

21
GOING HOME
(June 10–17, 2002)

THE FLIGHT FROM MANILA to Tokyo takes four hours. It immediately became apparent that more than a few fellow passengers knew I was aboard. As I was wheeled down the aisle, well-wishers reached out to touch me—some of them smiling, others in tears. The phrase I heard over and over was "I'm so sorry."

After another twelve hours in the air, we finally began our descent into Kansas City. As I looked out the window, I thought back to something Martin had written months before in the jungle in anticipation of this moment:

> Highest priority when getting home is to reconnect w/ the
> kids. Need to recognize and respect the role that others
> have had in their lives and not snatch them away. Our par-
> ents will also need some time. There are going to be a lot of
> demands on us, and setting priorities is going to be difficult.
> Sometimes we're going to do it wrong. Keep going.

What wisdom he had voiced!

A mixture of joy and apprehension swept over me. It was going to be so fantastic to see Jeff, Mindy, and Zach again! Even in my excitement, however, I was a little nervous. There would no doubt be some awkwardness once we were all together again. I had never worn

the title of Single Mom before. I hadn't even thought about what that would be like. I was bound to "do it wrong" sometimes. I knew that I could only ask God for guidance and not be too hard on myself.

I wasn't even out of the Jetway when I got my first glimpse of Zach, pacing back and forth. The instant I got out into the open, a burst of glee went up, even though there were strangers everywhere. I stretched my arms up from the wheelchair to squeeze Zach.

"I love you, Mom!" he cried, squeezing me back.

As I reached for Jeff, then Mindy, I exclaimed, "Oh, thank you, God! We're back together!"

I clung to Mindy and then I looked at her. She suddenly seemed very grown up. "I didn't know if I would ever hug you again," I told her.

"Me neither, Mom."

My mom and dad and Paul and Oreta were also there. It was so good to see them all again. We were quickly ushered into a separate room for just a few minutes. Along the way, I spotted friends from high school and college scattered in the crowd. I waved at them; it was so cool. I couldn't believe they were there.

After a moment or two of reconnecting with my family, it was time to face the media once again. Zach wheeled me out into the crowd of flashes and microphones. In light of the story I'd heard on the phone about his driving skills, I wasn't sure he should be the one to push me around with my leg sticking out. But he did fine.

Once again, I pulled out my card to make sure I said the proper things, and no more:

Good afternoon. It's good to be home. I want everyone to know that I'm fine.

Several minutes ago I was reunited with my children and my family, and I think this must be one of the happiest moments of my whole life.

We want to thank each and every one of you for every time you remembered us in prayer. We needed every single

prayer during our ordeal in the jungle. We know there were countless of you who don't even know us who prayed and offered support also. And we thank you.

I would like to thank Representative Todd Tiahrt and Senator Sam Brownback for helping my family and being such a support during this difficult time.

During our ordeal we were repeatedly lied to by the Abu Sayyaf, and they are not men of honor. They should be treated as common criminals. We support all U.S. government efforts in assisting the Philippines in ridding that country of terrorism.

A very bad thing happened to Martin and me when we were taken hostage. But we want everyone to know that God was good to us every single day of our captivity. Martin was also a source of strength to all the hostages. He was a good man, and he died well.

Again, it's good to be home. Keep praying for me and my kids as we begin to rebuild our lives. And thank you.

I was glad I'd written this out ahead of time. But even though I'd taken precautions like this, there were still a lot of inaccuracies in the media accounts of our story. The one that really upset me originated with the Associated Press and was picked up by *Time* magazine. They quoted me as saying of Martin's death: "That is God's liking. That is probably his destiny."* I would never say such a thing. In fact, this sounds more like an Abu Sayyaf comment than anything else. I wrote *Time* to protest the blatant misquote and got back a letter passing the buck to AP. The magazine refused to run a correction.

· · ·

We left the airport that day and were taken in a shuttle bus to a separate office building to meet the rest of our family. The only

*Verbatim, *Time*, 17 June 2002.

nonfamily member in the room was Rep. Todd Tiahrt, who had flown in from Washington for the occasion. "Congressman Tiahrt, it's a pleasure to meet you," I said, shaking his hand. "Did you happen to fly over Basilan on New Year's Eve?"

He looked a bit surprised and said yes.

"We saw you!" I said, and I briefly told him the story. He was amazed and pleased. It was fun to watch his face. He told me he was glad I was home and sorry he couldn't have done more to get Martin out safely.

I turned then to the family; we had so much catching up to do! We were all talking fast and furious, of course.

There was laughter but also tears, especially when I told a few stories about Martin's bravery and the struggles I had with God during my ordeal.

The more the conversation and celebrating continued, the more a slight divergence of mood settled in. Although my side of the family had lost a beloved son-in-law, they were primarily ecstatic at having me back again. The Burnhams, while glad to see their daughter-in-law, were having to face the aching reality that this scene contained no firstborn son and never would.

Oreta eventually came to me and quietly explained what was occurring. I hadn't picked up on it until then, but I definitely understood what was going on. I wheeled myself over to Felicia, who stood away from everyone else and seemed to be struggling the most. I held her hand as I said, "Felicia, I don't know how you must be feeling right now. It must be hard to come to terms with Martin not being here. But the honest truth is, I said good-bye to Martin over and over and over, every time the guns started up. He's gone now—and I can't stay sad. You didn't have him for the past year; you didn't get to say good-bye like I did. He was snatched from you, and I know it will be very different for you."

She gave me a hug, and we cried a bit together. In that moment I realized that I wasn't going to be able to please everyone in every

circumstance. I had to just do the best I could and, as Martin had written, "keep going."

In time we moved out into the afternoon sunshine, where a big charter bus was waiting to make the two-hundred-mile drive to Rose Hill. Everybody was talking at once. The kids wanted to tell me stories about everything from football season to the friends they'd made in Rose Hill to the Christmas musical at school.

As we left the Kansas Turnpike and got close to home, the sun was just setting. I began noticing squad cars with flashing lights at every intersection.

"What are these policemen doing here?" I asked my father-in-law.

"They're for you, to make way for the bus," he replied.

As soon as we got into town, I saw that the streets were lined with people! They were waving flashlights and holding signs of welcome. Others had candles. Yellow ribbons and balloons were everywhere. I just couldn't believe my eyes. I thought to myself, *Martin would be so honored to see how this town has turned out for us.*

When we got close to Paul and Oreta's house, streets were clogged with TV-station uplink trucks, and reporters were already talking into their microphones. I was helped off the bus and into a wheelchair. I waved at everybody across the street and called out, "Thank you!" as I blew kisses. *Those young, screaming girls must be Mindy's friends,* I thought as I smiled. As we headed inside the house, my heart was overwhelmed with people's kindness.

To be honest, I don't really remember much about that first night home—I was too jet-lagged. I can't even tell you who was there. I just remember being surrounded by people who really cared about me.

My family screened the visitors pretty stringently over the next couple of days, not wanting to wear me out. I heard somebody say, "Getting in to see Gracia is like getting into Fort Knox!" I ended up circumventing the system a time or two, sneaking some people into my room for visits when everyone thought I was sleeping.

My mom and dad stayed right next door at the Hansons' house. My brother, Paul, was there from Kansas City as well to help me start thinking through various financial matters, among other things. The living room was full of flowers and gifts and potted plants. The phone rang constantly. People brought food. It was amazing.

I looked once and noticed a woman in the kitchen who was not a family member; she was just quietly cleaning up, putting food away, and making coffee. It took me a while to realize it was Marilyn German, wife of one of the New Tribes Mission executives from Florida. She was such a servant. She hadn't waited to be asked; she just showed up and went to work for at least three or four days.

On the second morning, I asked Felicia to be my fashion adviser and buy me an appropriate dress for the funeral. I also asked her to do my hair and makeup for the next few days because I was obviously out of practice. She got a beautician friend of hers to stop by and put highlights in my hair.

• • •

The next few days were a flurry of activity as we made necessary phone calls and planned the arrangements for Martin's funeral.

I knew the speaker Martin wanted: his friend from college days, Clay Bowlin, now senior pastor of Northwest Bible Church in Kansas City. We used to pray for Clay every Sunday morning in the jungle, knowing it was Saturday night back in the States and he would be making his final preparations to preach.

Martin's cousin Kirk Hinshaw would play the piano, and Dan Smith, a soloist Martin had heard at Clay's church just before returning to the Philippines a year before, would sing.

I had assumed we'd have a small, quiet funeral at Rose Hill Bible Church, which seats maybe 200 or 250. Then somebody said, "Okay, now Central Christian has graciously offered their facility."

This is one of the biggest churches in Wichita, with a huge sanctuary. "It's kind of a big place, don't you think?" I said.

"Well, we're expecting about four thousand people."

I couldn't believe they were serious. Martin had been such an unassuming, normal guy. *He would be shocked at a crowd that size!* I thought to myself. But in fact, when Friday morning came, we found that we did need the space.

While others were making the various preparations, I knew I had a job that only I could do, and that was to get my kids ready for all this. They'd never really been to a wake or a funeral before.

It seemed that the only place we could really be alone to talk was in the car. I couldn't drive, obviously; I could hardly get into the car with my leg the way it was. But Jeff had his driving permit. So we all went down to Sonic, the local drive-in, for their famous Cherry Limeades. There we were able to sit in the car and talk awhile.

"Tomorrow night will be the viewing at the funeral home," I explained. "As you know, Dad really lost a lot of weight, so when you see his body, he's going to look really thin. And he'll have the beard you saw in the pictures from captivity. This will be the one and only time to see him, okay? At the funeral, the casket will be closed.

"The first hour will be just for us family members. After that, other people will come, and you don't have to stay for the whole time if you don't want to. It's just a time for making contact with lots of friends who have cared for us and prayed for us."

We negotiated a bit over what to wear to these events, like any mom and her sons would do. My sister Mary bought a really pretty dress for Mindy, and Felicia had helped me pick out a black dress with a black-and-white flowered jacket. Soon we were all set.

When we arrived at the funeral home, I was pleased to see that Smith Mortuary had put together an excellent video tribute to Martin, with pictures all the way from boyhood to college days, our early years in the Philippines, shots with the kids, shots with

his airplanes. The video told the story of his life and what it had meant, and it made us cry.

Martin did not look like himself. If I had it to do again, I would bury him in blue jeans and his favorite flannel shirt. Here he was all dressed up in a suit—and he never wore a suit. When we were home on furlough, he wore a jacket or suit coat only if he was going to speak in a church. He was just a very simple, plain guy.

I was shocked at how thin he looked—only 125 pounds, they said—and how old. I sat there in my wheelchair feeling so badly that all this had happened to him—a man who wanted the best for others and had given up the "American dream" to make a difference in a poor country. It didn't seem fair.

There was a bruise on his forehead that they hadn't been able to fix with makeup. *How did he get that?* I wondered. Had he gotten it falling out of the hammock? I didn't know.

But what I missed most was the laughter in his eyes. That's what *made* Martin—the twinkle in his eyes, the upbeat attitude that said, *No problem is ever too tough to overcome, no ordeal too grim to endure.* He had confidence; he was a doer, and he had fun in the process whenever possible.

The kids gathered around me and we cried together. They said, like family members so often do, "It doesn't look like Dad."

"You're right," I replied. "In fact, he's in heaven with the Lord Jesus, who he loved. This is just his body that's not working anymore."

I laid my hand on his hard chest and thought, *Poor Martin. You went through so much. You were so brave, and you kept me going so I could return home. I'll always love you.*

Soon people began to arrive—cousins of Martin whom I had met only a few times, friends from school, even a group of FBI agents from Kansas City who had been working on our case for months. They seemed so very nice. Many Rose Hill people came— even whole families—and said, "You don't know us, but we feel like we know you. We've been praying for you."

At one point, I looked around the room and realized our whole New Tribes team from the mid-1980s was there: Brett Nordick, who had flown on Luzon; Perry Johnson from Palawan; and Steve Roberts, our chief mechanic. "This was a good group!" I bragged that night, remembering all the wonderful times we had shared. The only team member missing was Martin.

It was late by the time I got to bed. The kids and I had decided to all sleep in the same room for a while. So Mindy and I took the bed, while the boys slept on the floor. I could lie only on my back because my leg was elevated on pillows.

We lay awake talking. "How are you guys doing?" I asked. We all agreed we were coping as well as could be expected. Soon they were asleep, while I lay there thinking once again about Martin—sad he was gone but oh, so glad that his ordeal was over and he was now in the very presence of Jesus.

• • •

"Are you ready, Gracia?" my father-in-law said in a low voice as he prepared to push my wheelchair into the church Friday morning.

"Yes, I'm ready," I said.

Everything else was in order, it seemed. The TV trucks outside Central Christian Church were already getting their signal from the pool cameras we had allowed to be set up in the sanctuary. The dignitaries were already seated: former Kansas senator and majority leader Bob Dole, now representing the U.S. State Department; Senator Sam Brownback and his wife; Congressman Tiahrt and his wife; U.S. Ambassador to the Philippines Francis Ricciardone; his counterpart, Philippine Ambassador to the U.S. Albert del Rosario; and others. Behind me stood the line of Burnhams and Joneses who would follow me in and fill up one large section of seats; the rest of the cavernous church seemed full already.

As we entered, the entire audience stood without being asked. I saw friends on all sides—from the mission, from college, from our

supporting churches, from places far away whom I never would have expected to fly in to be there. On the end of one row I spotted my friends Joyce and Kay, who had encouraged me to accept that first date with Martin so long ago.

Once my wheelchair was parked at the front, Zach took his place immediately to my left, then Jeff, then Mindy, followed by Oreta and Paul, then Felicia and her husband, Clint. Behind us came Doug and Teresa with their children; they took their places in the second row. The whole family processional took a long time while Kirk continued to play "The Old Rugged Cross." The familiar words could not have been more fitting for Martin: "I will cling to the old rugged cross / And exchange it some day for a crown."

One by one, various speakers and singers came to the podium, each one offering an eternal perspective on Martin's death. Central Christian's senior pastor, Joe Wright, commented that people often express their condolences at a time such as this by saying they're sorry for the loss. "We haven't 'lost' Martin," he observed. "We know where he is. And someday, because of the promise of God and the sacrifice of Jesus Christ on the cross, we can join him and be reunited."

Oreta's brother, Rev. Galen Hinshaw, gave Martin's obituary, which included not only dates and places but personal insights. The crowd couldn't help but melt when he got to letters written by the two older kids for this occasion.

The first letter was from Jeff:

My dad was a very special person to me. He would take the time to do special things with me. We used to take plane rides together. He flew me to Palawan from our home in Aritao. We were in a Cessna 180, so it took around six hours.

Once we were in Palawan, we visited all the tribes there. He

*said that one day I could fly for these people. He was going to
teach me to fly as soon as I turned 15.*

*He bought me a motorbike when I was 13. He taught me to
drive it and would help me work on it when I would crash it,
or when the motor needed work. I'm going to miss our times
together.*

Mindy had written:

*My dad was the most generous person I have ever known. Even
though we weren't a rich family, every time I wanted or needed
anything, he would do his best to get it for me. He was a big
family man. He never missed a chance to get away from work
and take our family on a vacation.*

*He would sing songs to me and change the words, putting
my name into it. He would sing them to me when he came
home from work and at bedtime.*

Rev. Oli Jacobsen, chairman of New Tribes Mission, compared Martin to the apostle Paul's associate Epaphroditus, who
more than once "came close to death for the work of Christ"
(Philippians 2:30, NASB).

"He was one of our best pilots, and one of our best test pilots as
well," he said. "As he trained others, his notable characteristics were
his patience and his attitude of 'you can do it.' One of our missionaries called him 'Mr. Cool.' But he was much more than a pilot. To
his fellow missionaries, he was a servant of servants."

When Clay Bowlin stood up to speak, I leaned forward. I didn't
want to miss a word.

"Why did this happen this way?" he asked, hitting on the very
question that had been gnawing at all our minds.

"I don't know. God doesn't always look at things the way we
do. Isaiah 55 teaches us that God's ways are higher than ours,
and his thoughts beyond our comprehension. There's a phrase

in Deuteronomy 29:29 that fits this occasion: 'The secret things belong to the LORD our God.'"

For the next thirty minutes or more, Clay had our rapt attention as he gave an eloquent tribute to Martin's life and work. He told college stories; he honored Martin's role as a husband and a dad; and in the end, he presented the gospel of Jesus Christ as clearly as possible. His most memorable line, the one quoted by news outlets afterward, was this: "Gracia was rescued from the jungle by a helicopter; Martin was rescued from the jungle on angels' wings."

We didn't want to end the service on a morbid note. There would be no filing past an open casket. In fact, we set the opposite tone altogether by bringing out a Southern gospel quartet to sing a song fit for a pilot: "I'll Fly Away." Toes tapped and people smiled as they prepared to leave the church after nearly two hours. It wasn't majestic or somber; it was instead upbeat and natural—just like Martin.

My heart was so full as I was wheeled out of the church. I wanted to stop and talk to so many people, but I couldn't. All that would come later. The family headed directly to a small country cemetery east of Rose Hill for a private burial.

My kids loved watching the Wichita police clear the way for us, blocking intersections and racing from the back of the line to the front repeatedly, light after light. We drove by a big Walmart with employees out front holding signs: "We Support the Burnhams" and "God Bless You Guys" and "Welcome Home, Gracia." Again, I was amazed.

Pastor Robert Varner of Rose Hill Bible Church conducted the graveside service, and then we soon headed to the middle school gymnasium, where the various civic clubs had prepared a huge spread of food for anyone who wanted to come. Somebody got me something to eat, but I hardly had time to touch it, because for the next several hours I was busy greeting people.

. . .

That night, the Burnham family gathered for a meal at the church. A little later, my side of the family showed up to do one of our favorite things: sit around with guitars and sing. I was amazed at how much Jeff's playing had improved over the past year. As the evening started to wind down and I got reflective, I thought that maybe I was truly weird in feeling that I had honestly "enjoyed" the funeral. I had seen so many people I loved. And the music had been excellent. Martin would have especially loved that.

When it was time to go to bed, we had trouble getting Jeff to stop playing his electric guitar. "Enough already, Jeff. It's late!" I finally announced. As we lay in bed, the kids and I talked about various things—nothing deep, just the events of the day. I reminded myself that I wanted to enjoy every day—whether sad or happy— with these kids. From now on we'd be together.

The next morning, Doug and Brian, Martin's brothers, plus Clint, Felicia's husband, made a flower bed in the side yard for all the potted plants and flowers we had received at the funeral. We put a stone angel we had received as a gift right in the middle.

Meanwhile, my family started packing up to leave. Several of them, however, stayed around for Zach's baseball game. Wheelchair or not, I was determined to be there. This was the kind of thing I had dreamed about for a year in the jungle—getting back to normal living and being a mom to my kids once again. The pageantry of the day before was fine, but the joy of watching my son play right field was every bit as meaningful.

My nephew Nathan transported me to the field, along with his mother, Beth. My cousin Sandy and her daughter Erin were there. So was my good friend from the Philippines Val Petro—the one who had taken the kids for "just a week" while Martin and I went to Palawan. Her husband, Bob, had passed away from a heart problem while we were in captivity. That led us to talk about heaven.

"You know, I just kind of imagine that when somebody arrives

in heaven," she said, "they make this announcement: 'Arriving at gate 42 in five minutes, Martin Burnham. Please proceed to gate 42 if you want to greet him!'" she said.

"Yes!" I said. "What a reunion those two had."

She continued, "I can just see Bob standing there and Martin saying, 'Bob! What are you doing here?!' Bob, of course, would already be in the know about Martin's situation."

Val and I talked about what we were going to do with ourselves now. She was thinking of moving to Indianapolis to help a new church get started. I told her I was going to stay in Rose Hill to raise my kids.

After the game, Nathan, Beth, and I drove back out the dirt road to the cemetery to see Martin's grave again. Looking at all the flowers, I felt great sadness at having to say good-bye to him. But I reminded myself that, just like the other good-byes in my lifetime, this was temporary.

I can't wait to see Martin again—and I will.

• • •

The next day was Sunday—an ordinary Sunday to millions of other people, but not to me. This was my first chance in more than a year to go to church. I absolutely could not wait.

So many Sundays in the jungle I had sat on the ground thinking of the high privilege of gathering with other believers to worship God. To sit in a pew (actually, in my case, they parked my wheelchair in the center aisle), to sing again, to pray, to listen to the Word of God—it was exquisite.

Doug Burnham led the worship that morning. We began to sing:

My hope is built on nothing less
Than Jesus' blood and righteousness;
I dare not trust the sweetest frame,
But wholly lean on Jesus' name.

On Christ, the solid rock, I stand;
All other ground is sinking sand,
All other ground is sinking sand.

My mind flashed back to the mangrove swamp on Basilan, where with every step we sank down into the ooze, where I longed for solid ground to walk on. I knew we had survived only by depending on Christ, the solid Rock of our faith and hope.

Doug also led us in Martin's favorite gospel song, "Wonderful Peace." This again unleashed a flood of memories for me—singing it in the dark as another day ended and we desperately needed God's calm for our troubled souls. How great to sing this song with a church full of people all worshiping the one true God!

The Scriptures that day were taken from James 1:2-4 (KJV):

My brethren, count it all joy when ye fall into divers temp-
tations; knowing this, that the trying of your faith worketh
patience. But let patience have her perfect work, that ye may
be perfect and entire, wanting nothing.

We also read from 1 Peter 1:6-7 (KJV):

Wherein ye greatly rejoice, though now for a season, if need
be, ye are in heaviness through manifold temptations: that the
trial of your faith, being much more precious than of gold that
perisheth, though it be tried with fire, might be found unto
praise and honour and glory at the appearing of Jesus Christ.

I sat there thinking, *Well, that's just what has happened to me.*
My faith has been tested, and I'm more sure of what I believe now
than I ever was before. God has given me joy and peace in the midst
of trials.

It was the neatest morning, worshiping the Lord and greeting the folks who mean so much to me.

There was one other gathering I knew I wanted to attend: the 6 A.M. prayer meeting on Monday morning. These men had been crawling out of bed and driving down to the church six mornings a week for more than a year now, just to intercede for Martin and me. I had to join them and say thank you.

I set the alarm for 5 A.M. Because I had to carefully consider every move I made as I hobbled around on crutches, everything took longer. Just getting past my two sleeping sons on the floor was tricky.

I was dressed and presentable a little while after 5:30. I made my way into the living room and gently eased down onto the couch. When Paul came out, he helped me outside and aided me as I hoisted myself up into the van. My dad joined us from next door, where they were staying.

At the church, I was wheeled in through the side door into the room where the men, Ralph, David, Pastor Robert, Les, and Mike, were already gathered around the long white table. I smelled coffee. They parked me conveniently at the end of the table.

So this was how it had been every single morning. These dear friends had held us up before God in prayer—and I knew that all over America and the world, for that matter, pockets of other people, prayer groups, and families had also been meeting to pray for us.

With tears in my eyes and a quiver in my chin, I began to speak. "Thank you so much for this act of love, which you've done over and over again for Martin and me. You got me home."

And then we started to pray.

22
REFLECTIONS
(Summer 2002)

LOOKING AROUND THAT CIRCLE of godly men, thinking about them driving to the church morning after morning regardless of the winter darkness, the summer heat, whether it was raining or snowing, in spite of busy schedules at work or home, I couldn't help but wonder: *Why did their many prayers—and those of thousands of other people—get only a partial answer?*

As my brother-in-law Doug honestly said to the media, "It's not the kind of reunion we were hoping for. We're one short."

After all, if quantity makes the difference in prayer, we certainly had quantity on our side. Six or so men praying six mornings a week for fifty-three weeks—that's more than nineteen hundred prayers. Add to that the intercessions of all the Burnham and Jones family members, our supporting churches across ten states, the entire New Tribes family of some 3,100 missionaries in twenty-five nations, all those who logged on to the Web site PrayThemHome. com, Martin's and my pleadings with God by night and day. The total is incalculable.

I don't doubt the truth of "Ye have not, because ye ask not" (James 4:2, KJV). But it sure doesn't seem to apply in this case; we all asked God over and over and over for protection and safe release. No one can say that our petition was inadequately brought before the Lord.

On the very next page in the book of James, it says, "The effectual fervent prayer of a righteous man availeth much" (5:16, KJV). Martin reminded me of this Scripture once when I was especially discouraged in the jungle. We were sitting on the ground during a rest break after hard hiking, listening to gunfire in the distance, and I was moaning, "We're totally forgotten. Nobody's doing anything to help us. Nobody's even praying for us anymore."

My good husband replied, "Gracia, you are wrong. Many people are still praying for us. And even if everyone else has stopped, our two dads are carrying on, I promise you. Remember what James 5 says about the prayer of a righteous man? We have two of the best."

He was exactly right, of course. The prayers of Paul Burnham and Norvin Jones alone would have met the requirements of this verse.

Obviously, the answer lies not in the number of prayers or the particular wording used in those prayers. There has to be another factor in the mix.

So what is it?

I can't claim to know for sure. There is an awful lot of Scripture that still mystifies me. During one of my many conversations with God in the jungle, I remember arguing with him about John 15:7 (KJV), one of the verses I had memorized as a child: "If ye abide in me, and my words abide in you, ye shall ask what ye will, and it shall be done unto you."

I said, *Lord, you would have an excuse if the verse included an extra clause . . . 'ye shall ask what ye will, and if I agree with you, it shall be done unto you.' But it doesn't say that!*

These things are hard for all of us. And in my case, it's not just an academic exercise. I lost a husband over this.

Perhaps it's useful to notice that while the verse in James says fervent prayer "availeth much," it does not say it "availeth *everything*." Why?

Because the Abu Sayyaf—and all of us—still retain the power of personal choice, the option of standing stubbornly against the

will of God. And that obstinate stance is, apparently, something an almighty God is not willing to bulldoze. Of course, he could have fired heavenly lasers into the brains of Janjalani and Musab and Sabaya, forcing them to wake up one morning and say, "Okay, Martin and Gracia, this has been long enough. Feel free to hike off whenever you like." But that would have made them puppets instead of independent human beings with free will of their own, for which they will be eternally responsible.

I find it helpful to think about this analogy: Asking God to free us despite the Abu Sayyaf's rigidity was perhaps like ordering the U.S. Marines to come get us despite a prohibition in the Philippine constitution against foreign troops ever again fighting on Philippine soil. This is a rock-solid law born out of four centuries of colonialism, first under Spain, then the United States.

Did the Philippines accept outside military advisers? Well, yes, although even this triggered protests in the streets of Manila. Direct combat? Never.

Since returning home, I've learned just how badly the American military wanted to launch a special operation for us! I've been told how they sat around conference tables in Zamboanga City just itching for the opportunity. They would, of course, have done the job far differently. They would have moved into action at, say, two in the morning instead of two in the afternoon, wearing night-vision goggles and all the rest to snatch us out safely.

A few months after my release, this is exactly what happened in the west African nation of Ivory Coast, when rebels took over several northern cities and threatened a school for missionary children. The Ivorian government in essence said to the French and American generals, "Go for it. Feel free to evacuate your citizens, and any collateral damage you do to the rebels along the way is all for a good cause in our opinion." Within hours the students and faculty were roaring down the highway toward safety, waving the Stars and Stripes out of bus windows.

But nothing like that happened in our case. The local authority

said no, and the Pentagon felt it could not trample upon an ally's national sovereignty.

Apparently, God runs into this impasse time after time. Having granted the human race a measure of self-determination, he would be hard-pressed to steamroller it when people misuse it. So it was with the Abu Sayyaf, and continues to the time of this writing, as their bombings and other violence keep showing up in the headlines.

· · ·

It makes for a messy world, doesn't it? Especially when radical members of a religion that accounts for one-fifth (more than one billion) of the planet's population feel called to advance their cause not only by persuasion but also by force and even terror. The extremist mind-set, as I experienced at close range for a full year, is not an easy thing to manage.

My experiences in captivity have made me think long and hard about an appropriate response to the challenge of the aggressive wing of Islam. I wouldn't presume to make any recommendations about public policy, but to my fellow Christians I feel compelled to say: We need to find ways to defuse the raging resentment and hatred that fuel "holy war" and introduce a God who does more than demand rituals—he truly loves us.

I am fully aware that millions of Muslims in the world are not bent on jihad. They are going through hard times themselves, performing their religious obligations over and over, hoping that somehow, someday, they will be acceptable to Allah.

For every hair that sticks out from under a woman's *terong*, I was told, she will spend a certain number of years in hell. People oppressed by such rules—not just Muslims but billions of people in the world who are desperately trying to stack up enough good deeds to outweigh their bad deeds so God will be happy with them—need our prayers. They need to know what it feels like to be forgiven. They need us to show we care.

When I was back in junior high, a popular song among Christian youth was "They'll Know We Are Christians by Our Love." It was the post-Woodstock era, the time when everybody tossed around the notion of love as the cure for all ills. I heard some adults ridiculing the song as naive and simplistic.

But in fact, that is exactly what Jesus said at the Last Supper (see John 13:35). People in today's world, whether Muslim or not, will not pay attention to Christians because we can explain our theology in crystal-clear terms. They will not esteem us because we give to charity or maintain a positive outlook on life. What will impress them is genuine love in our hearts.

Martin used to remind me of this while we were in the jungle. At one point, some copies of *Reader's Digest* appeared and we read them until they fell apart. Of course, Martin and I liked the joke sections. There was one joke about a teacher who in English class asked the students to write a story using descriptive words. Johnny turned in a paper that said, "The castle was big." The teacher returned it to him, saying, 'Big' is not a descriptive word. You can do better." The corrected story said, "The castle was big, and when I say big, I mean BIG."

We got a laugh from that, but a few days later Martin said, "I've been thinking about that story. Jesus said that if you want to be great in God's kingdom, be the servant of all. And when he said 'all,' he meant all. He didn't say be the servant of everyone but terrorists. Jesus also said to love your enemies. Do good to those who hate you. Pray for those who despitefully use you and persecute you." And that's what we started doing—praying for our captors, who were despitefully using us.

We have a chance to show the love of Christ to the world. I think Martin managed to do this successfully in the jungle. I'm not sure I did very well myself. I hope nobody calls me a hero, because I know the facts about the bitterness that blazed in my heart that year. I still have lots of maturing to do.

When you stop and think about it, the Abu Sayyaf are not the

only "bad guys," are they? We all have pockets of darkness inside ourselves. Recognizing how much I carry inside of me was one of the most difficult parts of my entire ordeal in the jungle. I already knew I was a sinner, of course. It's one of the first things I learned as a child in Sunday school. But I was also a missionary, a pastor's daughter, a lifelong "good girl." Weren't people like me supposed to be able to react to adversity with strength and grace and kindness and courage? Why wasn't I showing more of those traits?

I knew, for example, that I was supposed to forgive my captors, but the truth is that I often hated them. I despised them not only for snatching me away from my family and the simple comforts of a life I loved, but also for forcing me to see a side of myself I didn't like. There was a Gracia I barely knew existed: fearful Gracia, self-ish Gracia, bitter Gracia, angry-at-God Gracia. That wasn't the only me, but it was a bigger part of me than I wanted to accept.

Every once in a while, Martin and I talked about the fruit of the Holy Spirit as listed in Galatians 5 and how much we wanted to see love, joy, and peace in our lives.

"All I see is sadness and grief and sorrow," I'd say. "How can we produce the opposite?"

We learned that the fruit of the Spirit could not be drummed up by ourselves. We couldn't force joyfulness or loving action or a peaceful mind. The Holy Spirit had to grow those things within us.

I begged the Lord at times, "Please just give me some peace. I can't find it in my own heart. I can't find long-suffering. I feel anything but gentle right now. Please work some gentleness into my life. Give me some joy in the middle of this horrible situation."

And he did.

Now that I've come home to focus on my children for the next few years, I am determined to keep serving the Lord "with gladness," as Martin emphasized that last rainy afternoon we spent together. Some people in America want me to be offended and angry and bit-ter with the government for not doing this or that. Others want me to be depressed and morose—the poor, whimpering widow.

I can't be either of those. What good would it do?

What happened to Martin and me was no one's fault except that of sinful human beings, the kind we came to the Philippines to help. This ordeal went with the territory. I refuse to let this dampen my joy or detract from the love that God means to flourish in my heart.

Do I miss my husband? Absolutely. Every time I hear an airplane overhead, I can't help thinking about him—and I live next to Wichita, Kansas, the aircraft capital of the world. Boeing, Cessna, Raytheon (formerly Beech), Bombardier Aerospace Learjet, McConnell Air Force Base are all here. They constantly remind me of what Martin loved to do and did so well.

But no amount of pining is going to bring him back. I choose instead to rejoice in his memory and to keep it alive in my kids. One Friday night in August 2002, they were all at church for vacation Bible school and I wanted to go to the closing program. By now my leg wound had healed enough that I decided to walk the one block to our church rather than drive.

On the way I looked up into the wide Kansas sky, and for some reason, a deep happiness swept over me. I heard myself saying out loud, "Oh, Martin—you were the best! You were the best!" I don't know whether or not people in heaven can hear our comments here on earth. They probably have better things to do with their time. But if Martin was listening, I just wanted him to know how I felt. He was simply wonderful.

The special people God gives us along the way make us stronger to face the trials of an ugly world. Obviously, I never expected to face something of this magnitude. But I thank the Lord for helping me to endure it. I honor the legacy of a wise and godly man who kept me going, trail after trail, gun battle after gun battle. I value the efforts of all who worked so hard to get me out alive. And I resolve to keep living in the embrace of God's gladness and love for as long as he gives me breath.

23

BUT GOD MEANT IT FOR GOOD

(Fall 2009)

So much has happened in the years I've been home.

I'm glad to report that my leg wounds healed very quickly. Within a few weeks I was off the crutches and back to normal walking. As far as health goes, I had the most trouble getting the tropical amoebas out of my digestive tract. One medicine made me severely nauseous, so I stopped taking it. Eventually someone gave me a dietary supplement that helped solve the problem.

In the jungle, I used to console myself with every woman's fantasy: *I'm sure I must be losing an impressive amount of weight.* Well, would you believe that by the time my leg was strong enough for me to stand on a scale, I weighed the very same as the day I was captured? I was so bummed.

It turns out that all the exertion carrying mortars up and down the hills had burned fat but also developed muscle, which weighs more. I had certainly lost some inches, but no pounds.

The joy of my newfound mobility was immediately put to use. One summer morning about nine-thirty or ten, I got a sudden craving for a sweet potato. So I walked the three blocks over to the IGA and bought one. I brought it home, boiled it, slathered it with butter and brown sugar, and then sat down to have my feast! My kids thought I was crazy, but I didn't care.

A far more serious need at the beginning was finding a place

in Rose Hill to live. Of course, Paul and Oreta Burnham, Martin's parents, would have let us live with them forever. But I knew we needed to be on our own eventually. In the back of my mind, I thought maybe we could buy a modest trailer house.

Then came a letter from a local man named Steve McRae. He said he wanted to do something in Martin's honor. Plant a tree? That didn't seem big enough. What about the whole community coming together to build us a house? Would I be interested?

Oh, my. This was far beyond my wildest dreams. But the project began to take shape, and before I knew it, plans were drawn for a brand-new, nine-room home to be erected on a corner lot in the middle of town. People began donating supplies, cash, and time for what was dubbed "Gracia's house." It was overwhelming. We moved in the following February.

Meanwhile, a similar bolt out of the blue happened regarding a vehicle. Parks Motors in the nearby town of Augusta called to say, "Guess what—the Dodge dealers association of Kansas has decided to give you a van. In fact, it's sitting right here now on our showroom floor. Come on over and have a look at it. If you don't like the color, we'll reorder."

I was speechless. With no effort on my part, I was suddenly the owner of a brand-new Grand Caravan with all the bells and whistles.

When I had first arrived home from the Philippines, I had occasionally pictured Martin up in heaven, pulling on God's sleeve and saying, "Don't forget to look after Gracia and the kids. See what they need. Do you think you could provide that for them?"

Now I realized that the God of the universe didn't need reminders of what to do. He knew me and what I needed. He loved me. He bought my salvation. I began instead to think of God pulling on Martin's sleeve and saying, "Watch this! Look what I'm going to do for Gracia now. . . ."

The Lord has continued to supply our needs to this day, allowing me to concentrate on my mothering without financial worries.

The three kids began receiving Social Security checks, of course, due to their father's death. A number of our longtime donors have continued to support us, since I'm still on the roster of official New Tribes Mission representatives. The occasional speaking honoraria and book sales pay to keep an office going. God has blessed me with a wonderful assistant, Lynette, to manage phone calls and mail, which can be very heavy. God also brought along a retired pastor and his wife, Jack and Joyce Middleton, to handle booking matters. These three people have been a tremendous help, and I don't know what I would do without them.

THE KIDS

Probably the most common question I get these days is, "How are the kids?"

Well, they've grown up on me! Jeff graduated from Rose Hill High School in 2005 and already knew he wanted to become a pilot like his dad. Martin had promised to teach him to fly when he turned fifteen—but of course, that didn't happen. He ended up learning through other instructors, and the mission gave us the old Piper Super Cub that Martin used to fly on the field, which was due for retirement. Some missionary colleagues refurbished it beautifully.

So when Jeff left that fall for Liberty University in Virginia, I ended up driving across the country with all his stuff, *while he flew the plane to college.* Soon the university gave him a part-time job teaching in the aviation program, which paid his tuition bills. By the time he graduated four years later, he had climbed all the way up to a Multi-Engine Commercial certificate and Flight Instructor Instrument rating—the same achievements that took Martin many years. I'm so proud of my firstborn son.

He didn't spend all his time in the hangar or cockpit, however. Along the way during college, he told me of his intentions to marry another MK (missionary kid) named Sarah Neu. I knew her family and felt great about her character and commitment to the Lord—but, my goodness, these kids were still awfully young. Jeff

would be walking down the aisle at nineteen, while Sarah would be even younger.

"You know, Son," I said, putting on my wise-mother persona, "the culture here in America is that you get your schooling out of the way, you save some money for a down payment on a home or whatever—and then you get married. That's the way things are done here."

He stared me down with a serious expression. "Is that in the Bible anywhere?" he asked.

"Well, Jesus did talk about counting the cost before starting to build a house. You've got to be able to support a wife."

"Oh, I can do that," he affirmed with utmost confidence. "My teaching job is enough for us to live on. But here's the deal: *If I don't marry Sarah, someone else will.*"

I sat there thinking about the American divorce rate. Did our culture really have this all figured out? How could I truly object if Jeff believed God wanted him to marry Sarah? Her parents married young and have had a full life serving as missionaries.

The wedding—on May 27, 2006 (the fifth anniversary of our capture)—turned out to be wonderful. Ever since, this young couple has done so well. They're saving money and following God's direction the best they can. Will they end up working overseas in mission aviation? Time will tell. For the moment, Jeff continues to train young pilots at Liberty. He and Sarah are expecting my first grandchild in early 2010!

Meanwhile, Mindy finished high school early in December 2006 and headed off to a two-year program at New Tribes Bible Institute near Milwaukee, Wisconsin. She wanted a place that would provide good Bible instruction without putting her into major debt. The school has been a great fit for her.

She, too, discovered the love of her life while studying— another MK named Andy Hedvall, who grew up with his parents in Paraguay. Again, I was pleased with the selection. I did give him a hard time when he first called me to ask permission to date Mindy,

however. I said, "Well, you know, Martin used to tell the Abu Sayyaf in the jungle, 'I have to get home, because I have a daughter [who was twelve back then]. Someday boys are going to come around looking for her, and I need to be there to check them out.' And the Abu Sayyaf would always say, 'Yes, yes, that's very important. Don't worry—this will be over soon.'

"So, Andy, you have to make sure that Martin would approve of how you treat his daughter!"

In a somber and respectful voice, he answered, "Yes, ma'am. You have nothing to worry about."

Mindy and Andy will do well together. I am not worried about them. Andy is extremely relational, and I trust him with my daughter.

Zachary, my youngest, is the most like Martin. Sometimes I hear him in the other room laughing about something, and it's as if I'm listening to his father. He loves the Lord and isn't afraid to talk about him.

Zach finished high school in May 2009 and chose to take classes at a nearby community college. After hearing his great bass voice, the school gave him an impressive scholarship. And he gets to keep living at home for now.

Someone asked me not long ago, "As you look at your three kids, can you see any residual damage from being snatched away from their parents for thirteen months and then losing their dad in a violent, unnecessary death?"

I honestly cannot. All three of them continue to embrace life with a positive attitude. They love me, they love God, and they love each other. Both Jeff and Mindy are now starting to take speaking invitations from youth groups, women's luncheons, and the like. They excitedly call me afterward to tell me how it went.

AT THE PODIUM

Public speaking has become a steady part of my life, too, even though I never considered it to be one of my gifts. I expected some

invitations at the beginning, of course. The odd thing is, I'm as busy now as I was when I first got home. I counted up my engagements in the most recent complete year and found I had spoken (or given media interviews) well over a hundred times.

It seems like I keep getting invited to places I don't belong! Beyond churches and seminaries, I've spoken at veterans' organizations, cancer support groups, music concerts, jails, universities, philanthropist conferences, political rallies—even a yacht factory in Florida. One Rotary Club asked me to address "Terrorism in Asia: What's Being Done about It and What Is Its Future?" I took one look at that forbidding title and murmured, *Like I know that?*

So I massaged the assignment and gave it a new title, "The Future of the Abu Sayyaf," which I felt a little more competent to address. I set some background at the beginning and then told some jungle stories to establish my credibility. Eventually I said, "You know, there's a statement in Scripture that relates to this group of terrorists. It says, 'At the name of Jesus every knee [will] bow, in heaven and on earth and under the earth, and every tongue acknowledge that Jesus Christ is Lord' (Philippians 2:10-11, TNIV). I believe that someday that prediction will come true.

"Interestingly enough," I continued, "the future of the Abu Sayyaf is also your future. *Your* knee will bow, *your* tongue will acknowledge who Jesus is as well. The question is whether you and I will do so voluntarily or not."

I have found myself more than once at the podium of a conference on victims of crime. The planners seem to think I'm a poster child for that kind of event. In such settings, I do not rail against law enforcement, demand better access to justice, or call for harsher sentencing. Instead, I talk about forgiveness. "It's not something we do for the benefit of the other person," I say. "It's for you and me. None of us was meant to carry a weight of resentment and anger. We have to give it up to God, or it will crush us over time."

In front of these audiences, I also compliment the victims' advocates for the good work they do. I've seen it firsthand. These

are caring people who try to help a victim get through a horrible situation. After speaking I've even had government employees come up to me to say they're Christian believers—and they're going to be more bold to integrate their faith in what they do. "That's what will help a victim most," they say.

When I'm speaking to an openly Christian audience, I sometimes quote Ted Turner, the founder of CNN and one of the globe's biggest landowners. He was raised in a Christian environment but has openly turned against it. His line is this: "Christianity is for losers."

My response: And your point is? I'm not offended by the crack at all. We all have needs; we all need crutches. When a high school football player gets hurt during Friday night's game, he shows up at school Monday morning on crutches. Nobody laughs at him. Everybody knows he needs the help.

For some of us today, our careers are our crutches. Or our nice families. Or our good looks. Or our money.

In fact, Christianity is more than a crutch; it's a stretcher. It carries us where we can never hope to go on our own power. On that last rainy afternoon in the jungle, when the gunfire finally stopped, I didn't try to drag myself up the hill to the helicopter. I was more than willing to receive the help of someone's *malong* to wrap me up and support me. I thanked God for sending me assistance.

If I'm speaking to young people, I challenge them to consider going to the hard places of the world. "The easy places already have missionaries," I tell them. "It's the hard-to-reach, isolated places that are left. Some three thousand language groups have never had an outsider come tell them *anything*—they don't know the value of clean drinking water, let alone the gospel of Jesus."

I admit to the listeners that such places may not be very receptive, or even very safe. But God needs people to go there. As C. T. Studd, the accomplished English cricket player who turned his life toward service in China and then Congo, once wrote:

Some wish to live within the sound
of church or chapel bell;
I want to build a rescue shop
within a yard of hell.

We see the ongoing tension between the West and the Muslim world, and we wonder if it will never end. God has a solution for this problem. What is it? You and me! God gave us the job of caring for the world and bringing people to love Christ. There is no other plan.

Just how does he want us to deal with aggressive Islam? Jesus said it clearly: "Love your enemies and pray for those who persecute you, that you may be children of your Father in heaven" (Matthew 5:44-45, TNIV). Is there any way to exclude Muslims from what this verse says? Not that I can see.

I say to audiences, "My husband died at age forty-two. None of us know the length of the race we are running. We aren't told at the starting line. We only know that we must run.

"A tombstone usually carries a dash between the year of birth and the year of death. It represents the person's life—'the dash between the dates,' so to speak. And we get only one dash, not two or three. There are no do-overs.

"That is why we need to make our 'dash' into something that counts."

I am gratified to see growing numbers of young people responding to this call. When Martin and I were in the jungle, we used to worry that our misfortune had seriously hurt the future of New Tribes Mission in the Philippines. "Nobody's going to want to come here and do tribal work in the future," we moaned. "Everybody's going to shy away from this part of the world."

I am glad to report that we were dead wrong. Recruits are steadily streaming in. Young Christians these days, it seems, are not afraid of danger. The call of "Who's going to replace Martin Burnham?" has gotten a ringing response.

EVERYDAY LIVING

Even away from the microphone, I find people wanting to talk to me about the deep issues of their lives. Maybe it's just human nature that people are more inclined to tell their sufferings to someone who has suffered, too. Total strangers will come up to me in the grocery aisle and say things like, "You don't know me, but I know who you are, and I was just wondering if you would pray about my teenage daughter—she's really pulling away from the family." I've found I actually need to allow extra time for shopping trips because of this.

I've been asked for advice on tough problems that are far over my head: what to do about sexual harassment in the workplace, for example, or how to get over a raging anger. If I were God, I would not have chosen *me* to go through a year in the jungle or to counsel people afterward. I was obviously the weak link in our marriage, the ditzy blonde, while Martin was the strong one. Nowadays I can only share what I know and urge inquirers to go to the Source of All Answers.

Other times people come, not with problems, but rather with blessings. One June 7, the anniversary of Martin's death, I said, "Hey, kids—let's do something tonight that Dad would have liked to do. What do you think?"

They quickly proposed going out to eat, followed by a movie.

I said, "Well, I don't know that I can swing a *nice* dinner plus a movie for four. We'll need to eat cheap, okay?"

So we settled on Fazoli's, a fast-food Italian chain restaurant. The bill, as I recall, came to fourteen dollars.

We were sitting in a booth enjoying our pasta and breadsticks when a little girl about six years old shyly approached. She put some money on the table and began a little speech that was obviously rehearsed. "We want to give you this," she recited, "because we want to thank you for your service to the Lord." Then she bolted away to rejoin her mother in another booth. We all smiled and called after her with our thank-yous.

Zach unfolded the money; it was a twenty-dollar bill. The gears in his young brain began to turn. His eyes twinkled as he commented, "We just made six bucks going out to eat!"

But on other occasions, I relish just getting to be a normal person, part of the crowd of fans up in the bleachers of a Rose Hill Rockets football game, or a simple worshiper on a Sunday morning. My church family has really worked hard not to fawn over me. They let me be a regular member of a women's Bible study or a small group. I get to share my heart along with everyone else.

In the jungle, I always looked forward to Sunday morning, because it was the Lord's Day, and I would try to encourage myself, often by singing silently to myself. If we were hiking along the trail, I would sing something I heard Evie Tornquist-Karlsson sing long ago:

Walkin' to church on a Sunday morning,
   Walkin' and hearin' the church bells ring,
Seein' the folks who mean everything to us,
   Praisin' the Lord as we loudly sing.*

This was my treat. That experience still comes back to me now when I'm sitting in my church in America. I just love the experience of worshiping with others.

Any song that mentions *ransom* immediately grabs my attention. For example, Chris Tomlin's trailer to "Amazing Grace" says, "My chains are gone, I've been set free; my God, my Savior has ransomed me."† I'm so thankful that the ultimate ransom has been paid for my sins.

I can hardly contain myself whenever we sing the contemporary hymn "How Deep the Father's Love for Us" by Stuart Townend.

* "Sunday Mornin'," words and music by Kurt Kaiser, copyright © 1974 Word Music ASCAP. Recorded on the album *Evie Again* (Word, 1975).

† "Amazing Grace (My Chains Are Gone)," arrangement by Louie Giglio and Chris Tomlin, copyright © 2006 WorshipTogether.com; Six Steps Music (EMI CMG Publishing).

The second half of the last verse rises to this pinnacle: "But this I know with all my heart, His wounds have paid my ransom."‡

To show you how long-suffering my church family is: They've even tolerated camera crews from various news media trailing me. Some have ventured to the youth group meetings along with my kids as well. The locals just brush it off with "Oh, well, that's part of having Gracia with us. We don't mind."

Frankly, I have been amazed at how long the media interest has continued. To this day, it seems like they still come three or four times a year, usually in the wake of some world event that involves hostages being taken. I must be on their list to call or something. I'm going along minding my own business, and all of a sudden *Larry King Live* is on the phone wanting to set up an interview, or BBC News wants a quote. Then, of course, the local Wichita stations pick up on the exposure as well.

The UK branch of National Geographic came not long ago and spent three days at my house for its *Locked Up Abroad* feature. Oliver North came to film for his *War Stories* program.

It seems like when I'm the busiest—around Christmastime, for example—that's when the phone rings. I'm sometimes tempted to turn down the inquiries. But then I remember that these can be God-ordained openings.

WE tv, a cable channel for women, wanted to send a reporter and film crew to spend a day at my house. I said okay. Lo and behold, the reporter turned out to be a Muslim woman who had grown up in Istanbul, Turkey. We talked all day, it seemed. As we walked around the house, she asked me, "Where is a place that characterizes you?"

I showed her the window seat in my bedroom. "This is where I read my Bible in the morning," I explained. "I love the peace I feel here."

"Oh, we have to get a shot of this," she said to her cameraman.

‡ "How Deep the Father's Love for Us" by Stuart Townend, copyright © 1995 Kingsway's Thankyou Music.

When Zach came home from school, she interviewed him as well. Her heart seemed very tender. Zach told me later, "Mom, that's the first time I've ever seen an interviewer with tears in her eyes."

The group followed us to church that night, since it was a Wednesday. In the open comment time preceding prayer, the reporter even volunteered a prayer request.

Some of my Christian friends have said, "Gracia, what if these secular people misconstrue what you say? You can't trust the media these days, you know." But the fact is that in seven years of giving interviews to everybody from New York networks to Hollywood shows to international organizations, I've never gotten a raw deal. They've let me express myself the way I am. (In fact, the only time I felt my words had been twisted was, would you believe, in a Christian magazine. I'll never understand why they went hunting for some theologian to say I didn't understand the concept of ransom. Yes, I do—I lived the reality of that.)

GOVERNMENT GUESTS

When the first FBI agents and State Department men came to Rose Hill to interview me back in 2002, I gave them hours of time. But at a certain point in the afternoon, I bluntly said, "Okay, guys, that's it for today. I have to go be a mom now and watch Zach's baseball game."

"We'll go with you!" they announced. "We love baseball."

So we all went together. What a sight on the bleachers—four G-men in dark suits, white shirts, and dark ties yelling at the top of their lungs every time Zachary came up to bat.

Since then, various federal agents and lawyers have been back to talk, seeking any detail I might know that would help the war on terror. Even the Philippine government sent the acting head of its Department of Justice all the way to Kansas to interview me.

I'll never forget the day officials pulled out graphic photos of the terrorists who died in the same raid as Martin. There they were, spattered with mud from the rain; they looked awful. One

was Lukman, who had been so proud of the new T-shirt he had recently gotten. (He had given me his old one; I still have it and show it to audiences when I speak.) He died in that new T-shirt.

Another photo was of a guy who had *not* died in the gun battle. Instead, he was captured and beaten to death during interrogation. The cause of death read: "Heart attack." I scoffed openly. "Those kids were superfit, young warriors who could run through the jungle day after day after day," I told the agent. "No way did he have a weak heart." Then I started bawling.

The agent stared at me. "Gracia, what's wrong?" he asked. "Aren't you happy that these guys are dead now?"

"Well," I replied, pausing to wipe my tears, "if I believe what I believe, these guys stepped into an eternity in hell. God's offer of grace is now over for them."

Subsequent updates from John Gray and other FBI officials have provided news about the men shown on the "Wanted" poster (see photo section of this book):

- Abu Sabaya, our main spokesman to the media and the government, died in a gun battle at sea just a few weeks after I was rescued. What he never knew was that his "friend" Alvin Siglos had switched sides after learning that Sabaya had beheaded his uncle in one of the villages and was now working for the CIA. The new backpack Alvin had sent to Sabaya had a tiny homing device sewn into it, so that his every move could be tracked by the military.
- Hamsiraji Sali, who was part of our group but not as familiar to us due to his lack of English, knew his days were numbered. So he tried to work a deal to turn himself in to the American FBI, hoping his family would get millions of pesos as a reward. He also wanted to be held in an American jail rather than a Filipino one. In the end, it all backfired. He went to an AFP (Armed Forces of the

Philippines) checkpoint thinking he was turning himself in at the proper location—and promptly got shot.

- Khadafi Janjalani, the leader of the entire Abu Sayyaf, was shot in the neck while doing his prescribed Muslim prayers one night. His identity wasn't confirmed until months later, when a captive took authorities to his grave, and DNA testing settled the matter.

- Abu Solaiman, who always used to enjoy long philosophical discussions with Martin, died in a gun battle on my birthday, January 17, 2007. The phone rang early that morning at my house, and I assumed it was one of my sisters back east calling to wish me a happy birthday. Instead, it was my publisher's publicist wanting a statement for the Associated Press. The phone kept ringing all day from then on.

  I thought back to the day in the jungle when I had tried to tell Solaiman of the great blessing of Jesus paying for our sins on the Cross. He had sneered as he replied, "I'll pay for my own sins." Now ... that was indeed what was occurring.

- Bro (not pictured) was captured and wound up in a Manila prison. I was informed that he and up to a dozen other Abu Sayyaf attempted a jailbreak and were gunned down. Bro had always told us, "I don't want to go to hell. I want to die in jihad," which, according to his theology, guaranteed a quick pass to paradise.

CAPITOL CONVERSATIONS

Some of my dialogue with government officials has involved my traveling in their direction—to the state capitol in Topeka, for example (where I met Governor Kathleen Sebelius, now U.S. Secretary of Health and Human Services), and numerous trips to Washington, D.C. The first occurred back in the summer of 2002, when the White House invited our family and even the grandparents to a meeting with President George W. Bush. In a preliminary

phone call, President Bush said to me, "I'm so sorry that Martin didn't make it out, but I'm glad you did. How are you feeling?"

"I'm fine, Mr. President," I replied. "A lot of people who love me are helping me these days."

Entering the Oval Office was definitely an emotional moment. The president came over, greeted us, and shook everyone's hand. That caused my mother-in-law to choke up a bit, and Mr. Bush graciously put his arm around her shoulder as he began giving us a little guided tour of his office: the desk that dated back to Franklin D. Roosevelt's time, the big rug in the middle with the presidential seal on it, and so forth.

Of course, we posed for pictures together. Then the president said (at least as I recall his words), "I just want America to be a safe place, a place of freedom for our children as they grow up. And the only way that will be true is if we fight terrorism now. I'm going to do everything I can so our children can grow up in the kind of nation we've grown up in."

He also had a bit of welcome advice for Jeff, Mindy, and Zach. "Do you kids know how you can be a success?" he asked with all seriousness.

They shook their heads, waiting for him to answer.

He cracked a smile as he replied, "Obey your mother!" We all laughed together.

"Thank you so much for everything you tried to do for Martin and me," I said.

"Well, you're quite welcome," he said. "And there's something you can do for me. Pray for me every day, because I really need it. If a person working in this office doesn't realize his need for God's wisdom, he just really doesn't understand what's going on."

The same welcoming spirit was evident in the spring of 2009, after a change of administration, when the new attorney general, Eric Holder, designated me for a Special Courage Award as part of National Crime Victims' Rights Week. The Justice Department

attorney who first called me explained that I would need to spend three days in Washington for all the observances.

I knew him well from past meetings, so I forthrightly said, "You know, actually I'm booked to speak in California that following weekend, which is the opposite direction. So I'm sorry. I guess I can't make it."

There was a long silence on the phone. "Um, Gracia . . ." he said, "when the attorney general of the United States wants to give a person an award, that person finds a way to show up!"

Oh. I promptly changed my plans. I soon learned that nine others would be honored along with me. All the rest were people or groups who work *on behalf of* crime victims, including a rape crisis center in Boston and a group of six people in North Carolina who go after the well-hidden financial accounts and properties of criminals (usually offshore) so they can redistribute the money to victims. How had I landed in such an auspicious group? Jeffrey Taylor, former interim U.S. attorney for the District of Columbia, had read my book and put my name into the pot.

Amid nice meals and courtesy calls on senators and representatives, the first of two formal events took place—a candlelight ceremony at the U.S. Chamber of Commerce Hall of Flags that was open to the public. A large number of crime victims from the Washington area attended, along with several FBI agents who had worked on our captivity situation. Eric Holder gave a speech that night, followed by the lighting of candles and some musical numbers performed by a children's choral group. It was very touching.

The next day, a "by invitation only" awards ceremony was held at the impressive Andrew W. Mellon Auditorium on Constitution Avenue. One by one the honorees were called forward, each of them being introduced by a short video. Mine had been created by a West Coast producer who had flown all the way to Wichita to make it. Just ninety seconds of film, but it was very touching.

I was the last person to be named. When I came onto the stage following the video, Eric Holder pointed his finger right at

me and said, "You are the reason we're having this ceremony. It's people like you who make all of our work worthwhile." People stood and applauded as he handed me a beautifully crafted plaque that read:

SPECIAL COURAGE AWARD
presented to
GRACIA BURNHAM
for Demonstrating Extraordinary Courage and Heroism

I felt a little awkward getting a Courage Award because I'm not especially courageous. It would have made more sense if it were simply a Survivor Award. But I received it with gratitude nevertheless.

BACK TO THE PHILIPPINES

Travel to Washington was a mere puddle jump compared to the trip the State Department asked me to make in the summer of 2004. "Gracia, the Philippine government is getting ready to put eight of the Abu Sayyaf on trial. They need your testimony to strengthen their case in court. Will you go to Manila?"

I drew a long breath. "Well, I've always said I would do anything you guys ask. But will it be safe? I mean, I'm not interested in a one-way trip there, you know? I must come home to my children again."

"Absolutely," came the reply. "We will protect you at every turn. You'll stay inside the American embassy compound. We'll have security with you around the clock."

When I told the kids what was developing, they, of course, wanted to go along. "Mom, we got ripped out of the Philippines in a matter of hours when you and Dad were captured. We never got to say good-bye to our friends or anything. Can we please go with you this time?" they begged.

I aired their request with the State Department and was

promptly turned down. They said taking care of me would be a big enough challenge.

So off I flew to the Philippines accompanied by four FBI agents, one of whom would later act as my double. The minute we landed, they took me off the plane through a side exit so we would avoid the crowd at the end of the Jetway. But that didn't fool the Filipino media. You would have thought I was Jessica Simpson by the way they chased us through the streets those next few days. *Mrs. Burnham is back!* It was absolutely nuts.

Even inside the compound, I had to be escorted by armed guards from one building to the next. I did get to greet some of the NBI people (National Bureau of Investigation, the Filipino counterpart to the FBI) who had worked hard on my case. I met two guys who had delivered the ransom money to a warehouse. I thanked them for their courage. It was an honor to spend time with them.

The first two days were consumed with a trio of Filipino prosecutors and two U.S. attorneys. I knew them well because they had helped me get ready for my grand jury testimony in Washington. They all worked together, preparing me for court. I wanted to do a good job. But I was apprehensive. What if, when I actually saw the Abu Sayyaf in court, I fell apart? I prayed for steadiness when that moment came.

The morning of the trial arrived; it would be held in a small courtroom inside the prison where the men were being held. The media, of course, were breathless with anticipation, waiting at the embassy gates for my transit at nine o'clock. A big convoy was assembled and went zooming down the boulevard—but what the reporters didn't know was that I was not in the main SUV. It was my FBI double, acting as a decoy. In fact, it was she who showed up on the evening news across Manila that night instead of me!

In fact, I had been transported at five o'clock that morning, unnoticed, from the embassy to the prison and had already come in through a back entrance.

When I entered the courtroom, I immediately recognized the

faces of Bro, Ustedz Khayr, Bas Ismael, Daud, Jandul, and Umbran. I saw that the men had been assigned an interpreter, since the proceedings would be in English. My pulse quickened as I thought about their possible fate—the death penalty. This was a terribly serious day in their lives.

Fortunately for me, I didn't have to face them during testimony. In a Filipino court, the witness faces the judge, not the accused. The prosecutors walked me through a number of facts about my experience in the jungle. Eventually, however, I was asked to turn and look down the line of defendants, telling their names, the first time I saw them, the last time I saw them, what their job was in the Abu Sayyaf, and anything else I knew.

In two of the eight cases, I had to say, "Your Honor, he looks familiar, but I'm not sure enough to declare that he was with us. So I'd better not guess." The other six I knew right away. I began spelling out the details one by one.

As I spoke, their faces were not hateful toward me. In fact, Ustedz, whose English was quite good, sat there on the end of the row nodding his head! Whatever I said, he was signaling, *Yes, she's right about that.* Why didn't his attorney whisper in his ear to clam up? He was only incriminating himself, and nobody was helping him.

Finally, it was time for cross-examination. The judge announced that the defense attorneys could now question the witness.

The first query for me: "Mrs. Burnham, we understand that you say that during your captivity there was collusion between the Philippine military and the Abu Sayyaf. Is that true?"

The two American attorneys, who had sat quietly up to this point, jumped to their feet. "Objection, Your Honor!" they shouted. "The question is completely irrelevant to this proceeding."

"Objection sustained," the judge replied. "You do not have to answer that question. Counsel, please proceed with the rest of your cross-examination."

The two defense attorneys hesitated. Finally, one of them said, "No further questions, Your Honor."

What? I had come all this way, I had nailed their clients with all kinds of detail, and they had nothing else to ask me? This was going to be easier than I thought!

The judge was furious. "You have known for three weeks that Mrs. Burnham was coming here! And you have nothing to ask her? I am now calling a fifteen-minute recess so you can prepare some relevant questions!" Down came the gavel.

You would have thought the two men would have huddled to start writing notes. But no—one of them promptly headed out of the room to the prison gate so he could talk to the media. The other attorney, meanwhile, rushed to his car to retrieve his copy of *In the Presence of My Enemies* so I could autograph it for his wife. "She will kill me if I come home tonight without your signature!" he said enthusiastically.

I was upset. Even though these Abu Sayyaf had committed horrific crimes, they at least deserved a decent defense. They were getting no help whatsoever. My goodness, *I* could have done a better job for them. It would have been simple to say, "Okay, Mrs. Burnham, how many languages do you speak?"

Answer: "One."

"And what is that language?"

"English."

"Throughout your captivity, did the Abu Sayyaf converse with each other in English?"

"No, not really."

"Then wouldn't it be possible that you misunderstood a lot of what was going on in the camp day after day? How can you say such-and-such happened when the only natural English speakers in the group were you and your husband?"

They could have put a serious dent in my testimony. But they didn't think of that.

They could also have tried to say that the defendants were forced to join the movement through detention of their wives and children. I couldn't have made a very strong case against that; in

fact, it was often true. In other cases, I knew defendants had said things such as "The Abu Sayyaf came through my village, and I was 'sacrificed.'" What that meant was that their village had been invaded by several dozen fearsome warriors toting M16s and saying, "We need three recruits from this village—or else." To forestall widespread killing, raping, and pillaging, the village elders would offer up young men as recruits. It happened all the time.

I studied the court-appointed translators. They did virtually nothing. I knew these defendants didn't know enough English to catch half of what was going on.

I looked around for a court reporter, taking notes for the official record of the trial. I couldn't see anyone. But I did notice a little camera aimed at the witness stand. Perhaps this was their form of documentation.

The trial, as I said, was supposed to be closed to the media and the public. The little gallery seating area remained empty. But that night on the TV news, there was footage of the proceedings! Apparently someone on the inside had quickly leaked it to the media.

We sat watching back at the embassy. One attorney told reporters in all seriousness, "Mrs. Burnham has completely exonerated the Philippine military from any wrongdoing during her captivity." I had said nothing of the sort, either pro or con.

Soon I was back on the plane to America. I had done what my government had asked me to do, and the officials seemed pleased with my work. I kept waiting, of course, for news of a verdict and what the sentences would be.

Delay after delay kept occurring, however. A while later, the Philippine death penalty was eliminated by presidential decree, which gave me some comfort. At least men would not die based on my testimony. Still the legal machinations dragged on, and the men languished behind bars.

Eventually, a couple of them, including Bro, were killed in a jailbreak. It would not be until December 2007 that the rest would be found guilty and sentenced to life in prison.

SENTIMENTAL JOURNEY

As soon I got home in the summer of 2004, the kids, of course, wanted to know every detail. Their desire to go back themselves grew stronger. After all, they were as invested in the Philippines as I was; we said our family had now declared "a little jihad" in our home—on our knees. Whenever we read in the newspaper about the Abu Sayyaf taking more hostages or blowing up a building, we prayed that they would have the chance just once to hear the gospel of Jesus Christ in an understandable manner, so they could make an informed choice.

Mindy even began begging to transfer to Faith Academy, the MK school in Manila from which Martin had graduated. I didn't immediately veto the idea.

But I knew from experience that if we went publicly, the Filipino media would completely spoil our trip. I began making quiet plans for a getaway that Christmas. I didn't tell New Tribes Mission what I was doing, and I didn't tell the American FBI because I knew they would want to accompany us. I didn't even tell my family. I just went ahead and bought tickets. I notified one New Tribes couple in Manila and asked them to pick us up at a certain time—and not to tell anyone!

The first leg of our trip took us to Chicago's O'Hare airport, where we would go into cover-up mode. I noticed Jeff wearing a sports T-shirt that said "FCA" (Fellowship of Christian Athletes) on the front and "Burnham" on the back. Oops! "Jeff, you've got to change your shirt," I ordered. I then retreated to a restroom myself to put on an outrageously long blonde Farrah Fawcett wig that my assistant, Lynette, had found for me to wear. When I came out again and said to the kids, "Okay, let's head for the gate now," their heads snapped around in shock—they didn't recognize me.

"Mom! You're not gonna wear that!"

"Yes, I am." And it was a good thing I did. On the last portion of our journey, flying from Tokyo to Manila, I sat by a talkative Filipino man. He started asking questions—where did I live in

America, where I was going, and so forth. Then came the clincher: "What's your family name?"

I wasn't prepared for a question that specific. I stumbled around, finally admitting, "Burnham."

His face grew serious. "You know, a few years ago, there was a couple in our country by that name," he said in a low tone. "They were with the Peace Corps, I think. . . . They were taken hostage by the Abu Sayyaf. It was a really sad story." He launched into great detail from there.

I sat listening and holding my breath. Finally, he finished.

I had to make some kind of response. What should I say? I shook my head and murmured ever so slowly, "You know . . . I've heard of them." I then immediately grabbed a pillow and pretended to sleep the rest of the flight.

We got through immigration smoothly and met our missionary friends. They whisked us away and out of the city toward Aritao, where we had lived so long ago. There the wig came off, of course.

How special it was to be in this familiar place once again, after three and a half years. We went to the marketplace to buy Christmas gifts for each other. People were amazed to see me. "Mrs. Burnham, aren't you nervous?" they would ask me.

"What should I be afraid of?" I would reply.

"Oh, well, I guess there's no Abu Sayyaf up here."

We had a wonderful time. We bought supplies to give to nearby victims of a recent typhoon. We sang carols with them and listened to their tragic stories of loss.

It was good for the kids to be reimmersed in their former life. I could see them relax. They truly reached closure. The missionary family now living in "our" house invited us over for a meal. The kids walked around joyfully recalling the past. "Mom, remember when Dad remodeled this bathroom?" It was a wonderful evening.

The kids took long hikes up into the mountains. They spent one whole night there with some of the other MK teenagers, setting off New Year's fireworks at midnight. They hiked back the next day.

We showed up unannounced at the annual New Tribes conference, where NTM missionaries from all the different islands
gather for a week. My presence threw the schedule for a loop.
People wanted me to speak. They needed closure, too. Jeff made
up a goofy song for "skit night" and got everybody laughing. It was
all so good.

On the road back to Manila, we stopped at a large KFC for
lunch. I noticed people whispering to one another. Soon somebody
rushed to his car to get a book for me to sign. I ended up signing
napkins and posing for lots of pictures with people. It got kind of
crazy, and we escaped as soon as we could.

Finally, after three wonderful weeks, we flew home again.
Sometime the following April, the Philippine media called my
home to ask, "Is it true that you were here for Christmas last year?"
Yes, it was true.

A CHANNEL FOR GOOD

That trip, I hope, won't be my last—although security is always a
consideration. In the meantime, I'm constantly on the lookout for
ministry openings that the Martin & Gracia Burnham Foundation
can take up. I started this entity, on the advice of some wise friends,
shortly after I was freed from captivity and started receiving checks
from caring people. They had prayed for us throughout the year we
were in the jungle and wanted so badly to help—but couldn't. Now
that I was back in the States, their concern and love found an outlet.
They assumed I could steer the money toward God's purposes in
the Philippines and elsewhere.

So I defined four parameters for the ministry:

- Muslim evangelism
- tribal evangelism
- mission aviation
- the persecuted church

I also determined that we would put donations to work right away. In other words, we wouldn't try to create an ongoing endowment and just give away a percentage of the proceeds. If somebody gave ten dollars, we would send ten dollars out the door as efficiently as possible.

I was shaking hands with a lady in a book-signing line in Boston one day back in 2003, and she asked me, "How can I pray for you?"

"You know," I answered, "the last few weeks I've just had a burden for Muslim women. I don't know what to do with it. Pray that I'll figure that out."

"Well, do you know about Project Hannah? When you get home, Google it, and maybe this will be an answer."

I followed through and found out this was a ministry of Trans World Radio, a midmorning on-air "magazine format" program for women that gives child-rearing tips, recipes, and health advice, along with presenting the gospel of Jesus. It's aired in Muslim nations and all over the world.

So I called TWR and asked whether they aired Project Hannah in the southern Philippines. "Actually, we do," they said.

"What does it cost for a year?"

They gave me a figure.

I then called the members of our foundation board and got a quick approval. When I called TWR back a few days later and said we would underwrite this, there was a long pause on the other end of the line. Finally, the man said, "Right now down the hall, they're having a meeting about this. There's no money for preparing the Philippine edition of Project Hannah, and they're talking about whether to cancel it."

We've supported this project ever since.

We've also been happy to give to the Ibaloi translation project (Old Testament), the tribal group up on Luzon that Paul and Oreta Burnham served for so long. But we don't give to individuals;

we give to projects. And we certainly don't give to any Burnhams directly, even though we have several missionaries in the family.

I was speaking at a university in Arkansas, and the young man who planned the banquet told me his dad and Martin had been good friends during high school back at Faith Academy. "In fact," he continued, "my grandparents spent their lives translating the Scriptures into . . ." and he named the tribal language that many Abu Sayyaf speak. "They are retired now in the Dallas area."

I couldn't wait to contact them. I learned that much of their work was out of print. To me, that was unacceptable. I began to pray.

After I spoke at a church in Annapolis, Maryland, they gave the foundation five thousand dollars to print a series of thirteen "Lives of the Prophets" comic books that this couple had translated years before. The stories are about Adam, Abraham, Moses, David, Elijah, and on through Christ. They have proven to be very popular.

We also resurrected a set of morning and evening readings from Isaiah and Psalms especially chosen for Ramadan (the month of Muslim fasting). Again, the selections are keyed to prophecies about Jesus.

When we considered doing a bilingual dictionary for this language and English, we realized it would cost more than our foundation could handle. We managed to get a Tyndale House Foundation grant to help us on this one. The book is now being bundled for distribution throughout the southern Philippines with the New Testament and the comic books.

The most exciting recent news has been our partnership with a couple who minister at the New Bilibid Prison in Muntinlupa City, a maximum-security prison in the Manila area where a number of Abu Sayyaf are incarcerated. They conduct Bible studies, distribute literature, and do ministerial training of those who are genuinely converted and called to God's work. Nine of the prisoners, in fact, are now considered to be pastors within the facility.

The couple has given out copies of my book. One result has

been that these inmate pastors, who had shunned the Abu Sayyaf prisoners as despicable, have warmed up to them, saying, "If Gracia can forgive and love those guys, then we can, too."

Some of the terrorists who held Martin and me are now locked up in Muntinlupa—for example, one of the trio who broke into our resort room that first awful morning is serving a life sentence. I'm told he wants nothing to do with American visitors.

Another guy, on the other hand, is more friendly. He writes to me like a pen pal. He's proud of the fact that he "was once a cook for Gracia Burnham." I had to chuckle at one of his recent letters that said, "Even though I am here in jail, I has no fault; I am good." (Oh, really? This is the guy who beheaded a passerby one day and came up the hill laughing, with blood all over his yellow T-shirt.) He always signs his letters, "Your friend."

He has only one leg now, due to the fact that on the day Martin died, he was injured and couldn't keep up with the rest of his comrades fleeing down the river. They left him behind with five hundred pesos (ten dollars) to fend for himself. Three days later, the Philippine military found him. Gangrene had set in, and they had to amputate.

His story on all this today, incidentally, is that the *Americans* cut off his leg to keep him from running away.

But on the positive side: This man is now going to the Bible studies, although he is not yet a believer in Christ. The Bible study leader looked around the circle one day not long ago and counted up more Muslims than non-Muslims. At least three Abu Sayyaf have definitely come to know the Lord in this prison—perhaps more. I know two of them. Their change to new life in Christ is obvious, I'm told.

Granted, at first they took heat from fellow inmates, sometimes getting punched and hearing threats that their family members in the southern Philippines would be kidnapped if they didn't give up this new faith. As time has passed, however, those confrontations have lessened.

As one who spent more than a few nights of my own trying to sleep on the hard ground, I feel for the guys in Muntinlupa. Yes,

they're Abu Sayyaf—but they're still human beings. And they are souls in need of a Savior. I spoke to a group of senior citizens at a Missouri church who got interested in sending a large shipment of blankets for the prisoners—not so much for warmth there in the tropics, but to roll up under their heads for pillows. Each blanket was embroidered with "Jesus, the Messiah."

I talked with my kids about our family sending some of the men a little money each month—maybe ten dollars each so they could buy fresh fruit and vegetables in the prison's open market to supplement their diet or a pair of *tsinelas* to wear on their bare feet. They said, "Sure, Mom—let's do it." Some people in Western nations sponsor poor children with a monthly gift for food, medical care, and school fees; I guess we're "sponsoring" Abu Sayyaf prisoners!

I also instruct the contact couple to buy any handmade crafts the Abu Sayyaf make to sell, telling the guys that Gracia Burnham is their customer. This results in my getting boxes of these things to give away. I also send the men postcards of Kansas, so they can see where I live now. I am excited to be reaching out once again to the Abu Sayyaf and other Filipinos in a variety of ways. My kids are energized by this as well. It gives some validity to what their dad died for.

Everywhere I go, I ask people to start praying for these Abu Sayyaf prisoners. They are desperate and poor. Their neediness has caused them to begin looking to the Lord for answers. They have time to think about life and eternity.

There cannot be a harvest without seed planters. And the seed we planted in the jungle did not die. All these years later, we are watching God do something awesome, and we are amazed.

Martin and I lived among the terrorists for a year, separated from our loved ones. Only the grace of the Lord carried us through. Now the tables are turned; I have total access to my kids, while these Abu Sayyaf are shut off from their wives and children. The same Lord is waiting to give rest and peace to their souls. It is part of my daily joy to help make that connection.

ABOUT THE AUTHORS

GRACIA BURNHAM and her late husband, Martin, a missionary jungle pilot, served with New Tribes Mission in the Philippines from 1986 to 2001. Gracia now lives in Rose Hill, Kansas. She is the proud mother of three young adult children: Jeff, Mindy, and Zachary.

Gracia is also the founder and director of the Martin & Gracia Burnham Foundation. Because of her unique story, she is a popular speaker for churches, conferences, and schools. Her second book, *To Fly Again*, includes stories and reflections from Gracia that illustrate how God's grace enables us to rebuild our lives after heartbreaking loss and disappointment.

DEAN MERRILL is the author of seven books and the coauthor of twenty-eight others, including two with Gracia Burnham. He has also served as an editor with four different magazines and has traveled to forty-nine nations while working with International Bible Society and Global Publishers Alliance. He and his wife live in Colorado Springs.

THE MARTIN & GRACIA BURNHAM FOUNDATION

*seeks to extend
the Good News of Jesus Christ
through its support of missions
around the world.*

GRACIA BURNHAM

Founder and Director
www.GraciaBurnham.org
*For more information on the variety of ways
in which you may donate to the foundation, please contact:*
THE MARTIN & GRACIA BURNHAM FOUNDATION
PO Box 10
Rose Hill, KS 67133
(316) 776-0605
Fax: (316) 776-0709

The saga of the yearlong captivity of
Martin and Gracia Burnham
captured the world's attention.
People were amazed that they could endure such hardships
and even more that they could respond to their captors as they did.
What caused Martin to thank the guards
who chained him to a tree at night?

In the final days Martin and Gracia spent together
their thoughts focused on a passage of scripture that says:
"Serve the LORD with gladness: come before his presence with singing"
(Psalm 100:2, KJV).
Martin said, "We might not leave this jungle alive,
but at least we can leave this world serving the Lord with gladness.
We can serve him right here where we are, and with gladness."

Such attitudes are not generated by human effort.
They are a direct result of the grace of God in the lives of his people.
It is this life-changing message that
the Martin & Gracia Burnham Foundation
seeks to share with the world.

The foundation's goal is to provide funding
for special needs in the areas of
missionary aviation, tribal mission work,
Christian ministries to Muslims, and
the often-neglected persecuted church around the world.

The horrendous ordeal is over for Martin and Gracia Burnham.
Though Martin is now with the Lord,
his message is far from being extinguished.
You can help continue the legacy of faith that Martin embraced
and extend the good news of the wonderful love, faithfulness,
and saving grace of Jesus Christ
to a world that desperately needs to know him.

Online Discussion
guide

TAKE *your* TYNDALE READING
EXPERIENCE *to the* NEXT LEVEL

A FREE discussion guide for this book
is available at bookclubhub.net, perfect
for sparking conversations in your book
group or for digging deeper into the text
on your own.

www.bookclubhub.net

*You'll also find free discussion guides for
other Tyndale books, e-newsletters, e-mail
devotionals, virtual book tours, and more!*

"A training manual for anyone seeking to fly above discouraging circumstances."
MAX LUCADO

TO *Fly* AGAIN

Surviving the Tailspins of Life

GRACIA BURNHAM
WITH DEAN MERRILL

The world learned the horrendous details of Martin and Gracia Burnham's yearlong captivity in *In the Presence of My Enemies*. *To Fly Again,* Gracia's reflections on the lessons and spiritual truths she learned in the jungle, squarely addresses the challenges each of us face when we lose control of some aspect of life. This book offers no pat answers or easy solutions, just the battle-tested wisdom of a woman who lived her greatest nightmare and came through it more convinced of God's grace than ever before.

978-1-4143-0125-9 (softcover)

From best-selling author
STEVE SAINT

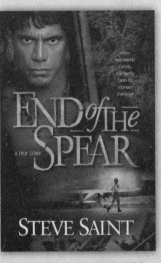

Over 100,000 copies sold!

Steve Saint was five years old when his father, missionary pilot Nate Saint, was speared to death by a primitive Ecuadorean tribe. Years later, when that same tribe asks Steve for help, Steve, his wife, and their teenage children move back to the jungle. There, Steve learns long-buried secrets about his father's murder and finds himself caught between two worlds. *End of the Spear* brilliantly chronicles Steve's continuing role in the most powerful missionary story of the twentieth century.

Don't miss the gripping major motion picture from Every Tribe Entertainment.

978-0-8423-8488-9 (softcover)

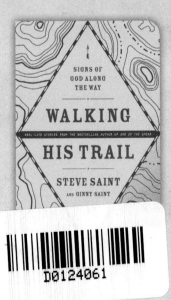

Steve Saint returns with a series of adventurous, inspiring stories of how God makes himself known through both the dramatic and the seemingly mundane events of life. While walking God's trail all over the world, Steve has spotted the Creator's hand at work in many significant life moments—from finding the love of his life to befriending the tribe that murdered his missionary father; from living in the Ecuadorean jungle to creating a major motion picture and presenting it before the United Nations. Sometimes triumphant, sometimes tragic, Steve's invariably thrilling tales are those of a born storyteller.

978-1-4143-1376-4 (softcover)

CP0136